# MEAL PREP MADE EASY

## DEDICATION

This book is for you.

You, who have picked this up and given me a chance to change the way you work in the kitchen. You, with real life commitments, a social life, a family, and probably zero time to really be reading this (did you feed the dog?). I'm so happy you're here, prioritising something just for you.

Like you, I'm juggling a million things: a busy nutrition clinic, a social life, my mental health, working out, travelling. Yada yada yada. There've been moments when I've mastered it all, and moments when I've royally — and publicly — failed.

My challenge for you is to eat wholefoods 80 per cent of the time, and enjoy the rest. This method is the backbone of my nutrition business, and I can proudly report that after serving thousands of women, you CAN stop overeating. If you want your meal prep customised for your body composition goals, come join me for your personalised meal plan at www.status8020.com.

I am so incredibly grateful to every subscriber, follower, reader and friend who has supported me on this journey. You've read my many ramblings (including this one), and I dig it that I can offer something back to you in the following pages. Even if it really is just an enthusiastic smile and a delicious quiche.

Thank you for helping me create a career beyond my wildest dreams.

*Sally*

@sallyoneil

DISCLAIMER: The content presented in this book is meant for inspiration and informational purposes only. The purchaser of this book understands that the author is not a medical professional, and the information contained within this book is not intended to replace medical advice or to be relied upon to treat, cure or prevent any disease, illness or medical condition.

# MEAL PREP MADE EASY

High-protein batch cooking recipes: featuring nutritional advice for healthy eating and meal planning 101

## Sally O'Neil
BHSc Nutritional Medicine and Dietetics

murdoch books
Sydney | London

# Contents

**Meal prep 101**     6

**Step 1: Prep your protein**     38

Learn how simple it is to cook the star of the plate: meat, fish, poultry and vegie proteins are the starting point of your meal.

**Step 2: Batch and stash**     76

More than 35 easy recipes to batch make. Get that pantry, fridge and freezer stocked for the week ahead.

**Step 3: Put it together**     150

Over 75 different combo plates that mix and match. Never run out of mealtime ideas again.

MEAL PREP 101

# Let's make this simple

Even with a lovely home office, I'm sitting writing this at a slightly sticky table in my local library, with a group of noisy children as the backing track. Why? Because I get distracted by stuff. Life stuff that I'm sure you deal with too: washing, phone calls, reorganising the spice rack 30 times a year, the rude call of Netflix. We're ALL trying to figure out how to do life — a happy, healthy life — and do it with some balance.

Let's be honest, being healthy can be pretty time-consuming. All that yoga, hours at the farmers' markets, squeezing your own green juices, and then meal planning is all a bit much. When time is in short supply, all of this can get pushed into the back seat. Even as a Clinical Nutritionist, I can't honestly say that I cook myself a meal from scratch every night. I've got shit to do, and that doesn't involve spending hours at my stove.

While I am single-handedly running a busy clinic, completing specialised studies in Women's Health Medicine, creating content for Status 8020 (my online coaching platform) and trying to explore more of the world, I also want to take care of my body. I want to feel good while I tackle my to-do list and I know you do too, but sometimes that goal can feel pretty elusive. So while I haven't got all the answers, I'm here to share my favourite food hacks: the tricks and tips I've learned that make healthy food SIMPLE.

My method is this: prep it, batch it, store it, assemble it. Okay, the prep might take a bit of time (we're talking 2 hours a week, tops), but, short of ordering meal delivery every night, you're not going to find a faster way to eat home-cooked, healthy food. This is the shortcut. This un-cooking cookbook aims to help you claw back time for actually important life stuff.

Now, we're wasting valuable time. In the words of the great Macklemore: let's eat.

*Sally* x

MEAL PREP 101

# Why meal prep?

We all seem to have less and less time, and when we're pressed for time the first things to go are sleep and cooking. While I can't help you out with getting more Zs, I can save you time AND money by teaching you the foundations of meal prep.

We seem to get by on less sleep and more coffee, less cooking and more takeaway. The end point is the same, but quality of life takes a hit. What you put into your mouth has a huge effect on your weight and physical health. Exercise is an awesome way to improve things, but it can't undo a bad diet. Eating well improves your mental health as well; when you eat good food you feel better about your choices and happier with the way your body feels.

Healthy meals need to be easy to prepare and readily accessible if you want to have a chance of sustaining a balanced, nutritious diet. Once you have a few simple cooking methods and systems under your belt, endless meal combinations will be open to you.

I'm a passionate advocate of prepping food for the week ahead. When I talk about prepping, I don't mean spending your entire weekend making 'all the things'. What I am talking about is the intentional action of making a couple of hero foods that can be used in multiple dishes throughout the week. Every now and then I make other things in bulk, so that I can freeze them, ready to pull out whenever I need. If you can get into the bulk-cooking mindset, you'll begin to spend less time in the kitchen, yet have more food ready to eat in your fridge or freezer when you need it.

When I started planning meals with wholefoods, I felt overwhelmed. It wasn't until I learned to cook some hero proteins (Step 1), created recipes that I could batch-make and stash (Step 2), and then learned the art of 'food assembly' (Step 3), that I managed to get plenty of variety into my diet with minimal cooking time. I'm definitely not going to win any awards for reinventing the cooking wheel, but I sure as hell can teach you how to turbocharge your meal prep to work faster and smarter.

If you want fine-dining options to wow your highbrow guests, you've picked up the wrong book. Go see a celebrity chef and set aside a day with your dry-ice packs. Meal planning isn't about creating super-fancy or impressive meals every night; it is about cutting down your daily cooking time and taking back those precious minutes for the important stuff, while still eating well.

### Five benefits of meal prep

1. Saves time
2. Saves money
3. Reduces waste
4. Keeps your health on track
5. Helps with portion control

MEAL PREP 101

# How to put it all together

To save your sanity, you're not going to be batch-making almond milk and raw nut butters, soaking your own legumes, or making other things you can access easily and cost-effectively from a store. There's also no place here for anything dehydrated, house-fermented or with a million superfood ingredients. It's a headache, time-consuming and super-frustrating if it's just not your jam. Burning precious time in the kitchen is not the aim of the game here. This is fast-action food assembly.

### What's meal prep about?

The goal of meal prep is to cook food in advance so that you can assemble meals with little to no effort during your busiest times of the week. Rather than cooking oats every morning, you prepare five servings in one go to last you the entire working week. It saves you a heap of time when you're at your busiest, and also stops you from reaching for unhealthier options.

Some people love to portion out their meals ready to grab and go, whereas others are keen for a little assembly when hunger strikes. Either way, you'll be making your time in the kitchen far more efficient and saving time for stuff that really matters.

There's nothing stopping you from popping to the shops for a decent ready-made pesto or a jar of pickles. SHORTCUTS ARE OKAY. In fact, I've listed some of my fave Supermarket Saviours on pages 28–29. Everything here is optional and designed to make healthy eating as simple and tasty as possible throughout your working week.

A lot of recipes in this book offer two or three options. That's because once you've mastered the basics, I want you to be inspired to try assembling them in different ways. It's timesaving and avoids the dreaded food fatigue from eating the same thing three days in a row. YAWN.

IT REALLY IS AS SIMPLE AS ...

Step **1** → Step **2** → Step **3**

You're going to start by prepping the main event — the yummiest bits of the dish — in Step 1. This is where you really learn the skills for prepping a few good basics that can be used over and over.

Step 2 will have you batch-baking and making snacks and meals that can be eaten straight away, or refrigerated and frozen for later use.

Step 3 is where you'll get inspo to put all of this together into a zillion combos so you'll never have to eat the same dish night after night. It's called food assembly, because that's all you're required to do.

*Shortcuts are okay! See pages 28-29 for some of my faves.*

MEAL PREP 101

# Getting started

You know those people who can rustle up an amazing meal when their fridge is seemingly empty? That's the future you. Hey there, resourceful culinary genius!

Making a meal plan might sound like a time drain when you're super-busy. I get it: but trust me when I say it's one of the most impactful ways of organising your life. Here are some quick and simple ways to improve your meal-planning prowess.

## 1

**STOCKTAKE**

Run to your pantry, fridge and freezer and take note of what you already have.

## 2

**SELECT + TEXT**

Flip through this book and add a few sticky notes (or just fold the corners … I'll never know) on the recipes you already have ingredients for. If you're missing a few key things, text a quick list to yourself so you can remember what you need next time you go shopping. If you have some key ingredients but are just missing the inspo to put it together, then head to Step 3 of this book.

## 3

**WRITE IT DOWN**

Grab a notebook (see Tip) and write out the days of the week, then write down your meal ideas using the food you have on hand. Make sure to include a 'leftovers buffet' night to eat up anything that's left. You can always throw in a tin of tuna or a hard-boiled egg to make it a more complete meal. Congrats — you just did your meal planning!

**Tip**

Use a notebook to make your meal plans; avoid using (s)crap paper, or you'll end up losing your hard work. Your notebook will be your goldmine for ready-made meal plans. As you go along, you'll refine them to include your fave options and those that work best for your time allowance. Ideally, you'll learn 15-30 delish, hardworking recipes that you'll use as staples, mixing it up with a few newbies every so often so you can avoid food fatigue.

In the art of working smarter, not harder, you can reuse these meal plans on rotation. More time saved!

# 4

## MAKE TIME

Allocate some time in your diary to prep and store your key ingredients. If you only have five minutes to chop vegies, do that.

Scribble in your notebook what prep is required, starting with the most time-consuming tasks first. I find this helps keep me focused in prep time and gives me an efficient work flow: what to make first, second, and last.

# 5

## COOK ONCE, EAT TWICE

Whenever you prep something by mixing, blending or adding heat, you're going to make more than one portion... always.

Most of the meals (or the components of them) in this book are freezable or will last up to a week in the fridge. This ensures that you won't get bored. Food fatigue is a real thing, and it will derail your efforts. That's why assembly of different food combos and dressings are so important. But more on that in Step 3.

# 6

## ENJOY YOUR SPARE TIME

As well as knowing that you've got a lot of healthy meal options ready to go, you just bought yourself a whole lot of extra leisure!

*It always helps to have a clean kitchen with your meal-prep containers washed and ready to go.*

MEAL PREP 101

# Tips for success

These are a few things I've learned about planning ahead that will definitely make your meal prep easier.

### Start small
Please don't flip over to the next few pages and feel overwhelmed by the need to make eight different recipes for the week ahead. Start small, and multitask. If you have a spare 10 minutes (come on, I know you do), you have time to prep your breakfasts for the entire week with a big batch of overnight oats, Work with the time you have, and the ingredients you have.

Try by picking a few simple recipes without many ingredients and whatever you don't have in the house, stick on a shopping list. You'll find it easier if you pick a few recipes that utilise the same ingredients, and it saves on food waste too. You'll get the hang of this quickly.

### Keep it simple
If I were here to tell you how to make extravagant meals, you'd be hatin' on me for the time and cost involved. Simplicity is our key focus. That doesn't mean bland, repetitive food, but it does mean getting into the habit of preparing ingredients simply and then amping up flavour with sauces, herbs and a bit of imagination. To make sure you have plenty of variation, we'll focus on perfecting the main protein event of meals — think chicken, fish, tofu — and then learn how to assemble these super-quickly in a number of different ways so you don't get sick of the same stuff.

### Get creative
Experiment with swapping ingredients listed in the recipe for what you have available: whatever's in season, your favourite vegies, or what's in your pantry. I am not asking you to go out and buy a whole new pantry of ingredients, I'm trying to help you save money and time — not spend more of both. If a recipe calls for dried oregano, and you only have paprika, just switch it!

### Multitask
Pick recipes with different cooking methods so you can multitask. That way, something can be baking in the oven while you're poaching something else on the stovetop. Start on the stuff that takes longest to cook and finish with the simplest prep. You'll save a lot of time this way and get more food prepped!

Roast different foods with the same cooking time together. Pairing root vegies (those that are grown underground), such as carrots, sweet potato and parsnips, in the same roasting tray can save time and add variety. Fast-cooking veg (usually softer and grown above ground) can be paired too: think asparagus, cherry tomatoes and zucchini.

### Don't be afraid to take shortcuts

Contrary to popular belief, you're not actually superwoman. There are some things you just won't have time for, and when that time comes, there's no need to beat yourself up for taking a shortcut. I've listed some of my timesaving tips on pages 24–25.

### Masterclass

Instead of attempting to cook entire meals, the focus of this book is to break them down into common parts that you can cook separately and ahead of time. This means you can mix and match buffet-style and really focus on combining different foods at each meal. We'll get into this in Step Three, where you'll be looking to pick foods from different categories (carbs, fats and proteins) to make a balanced, complete meal.

> *If you're new to this, start by prepping just a few days' worth of meals.*

MEAL PREP 101

# Nutrition 101

Before you dive into DIY Kingdom and start to prep your meals like a boss, you need to know how to build a balanced meal. 'Balance' refers to the type and amount of macronutrients on your plate. There are three macros you need to include in each meal, and they all serve a different purpose.

It's highly likely you're going to flip through this cookbook, like many others that have graced your hands before it, for meal inspiration. You want pretty food pictures, some easy tips on saving time, and a couple of winning healthy dinner ideas that you can rustle up on the fly. You'll then go into the kitchen and decide what is most convenient to make with one of my ideas as a loose plan for the dish.

That's perfect. This isn't a dogmatic recipe guide or diet. You're nailing meal prep if you want to go it alone and DIY – it means you're integrating it into your life as a good habit on the regular and are willing to get creative. Not eating the same thing every day is the only way a meal prep system will work for you. Variety is the key to success (and the spice of life, obvs). It's better for your body, too, when you're packing in a wider range of vitamins and minerals from different foods rather than sticking to the same stuff. #EatARainbow and all that.

So what are the three macronutrients and how do you include them in your diet? They are carbohydrates (carbs), proteins and fats.

Why do we need all three in a meal for balance? In essence, it's related to how quickly your body burns through them. The quickest to break down (or burn) are carbs, then proteins, with fats being the slowest. If you really want to get into that, read on. I love to be armed with all the info so I can make the best of every meal, and it makes it easier to choose a healthy, satisfying meal when you eat out (or order in).

## Carbs

Your body burns carbohydrates first – they are broken down into glucose in the body to provide its primary source of fuel. Not all carbs are created equal. There are subcategories (are you zoning out yet?) of 'Simple Carbs' and 'Complex Carbs'. Simple carbs burn faster than complex, because they've only got one or two chemical bonds holding their structure together. Oooh, this is like a science lesson ... you're SO welcome.

White sugar is one such simple carb. It actually starts out as brown sugar. MIND BLOWN? When the molasses is removed, the simple sugar crystals are left. White rice is another simple carb, with the bran and germ removed from its original brown-rice state. Natural simple carbs exist, too: certain vegies (white potato, I'm looking at you), some fruits and milk.

When you eat a simple carb, it's broken down super-fast and the glucose is funnelled into the blood stream quickly. A rush of glucose hits your blood stream = hello blood-sugar spike! On the other hand, complex carbs (often referred to as 'good' carbs) are the ones that take longer for your body to digest and break down. Think sweet potato, whole grains (like brown rice), steel-cut oats and pumpkin. Chemically, they have three bonds to break down, which just takes longer. That means blood-sugar levels remain more stable as a result because the glucose is slower to reach the bloodstream.

Okay, enough of that. Let's just say complex carbs are your mates. Simple carbs less so. Limit them where you can, but also, don't be insane. Cow's milk isn't going to kill you. (Unless it's off. Tip: don't store milk in a hot car.)

## Proteins

Next up in the fuel-burning tank is protein. Proteins have a more complicated structure than carbs, being composed of many little building blocks called amino acids. Protein bonds need acid to break them because they're difficult to denature. That's why we have some lovely hydrochloric acid in our stomachs to mix around with our food to break them down. Protein is loved by gym-goers and dieters alike, primarily because it helps with muscle repair. A higher muscle ratio in the body means a higher basal metabolic rate (your metabolism rate at rest) and therefore more calories burnt doing absolutely nothing more than the average person. It's really a lot more complicated than that, but for now we just need to know that adequate protein is important to keep us healthy.

## Fats

Fat takes the longest to digest and helps to delay stomach emptying: we stay full for longer! It's also the highest kilojoule count per gram, so we don't need heaps of it to sustain us. It helps our bodies make use of any fat-soluble vitamins we eat. Without the fat, as the name suggests, these vitamins (namely A, D, E and K) become difficult for our bodies to use – so think of fat as a tasty vitamin carrier, if you will. Without going into the science of fats because, well, your life is passing you by, let's just say there are some fats that are better for us than others. Generally speaking, unsaturated fats are better for us than the saturated kind. (There's a bit of a debate about coconut oil, but you can do some research on this for yourself, using reputable sources. I like to use it in baking where it adds flavour and texture.)

### CARBS
**Primary digestion location:** begins in the mouth (with saliva) and continues in the stomach.

---

Totally demonised in recent years by the keto movement, and prior to that the Atkins Diet, carbs really do get a bad rap. They are, however, your body's primary source of fuel and your brain needs them to function, peeps. In fact, your alertness and concentration depend on them. You'll get them from starchy veg, brown rice, sourdough bread, oats, and the like. Don't be a carbophobe.

### PROTEINS
**Primary digestion location:** stomach.

---

Protein is the main component of muscles, bones, skin and hair. Protein burns more calories when it is digested because the chemical bonds are a bitch to break down. It increases the production of two hormones that help you feel full and satisfied, and it also reduces the hunger hormone. Double win. Find it in meat, oats, seafood, tofu, nuts, protein powder (surprise!), beans and other legumes.

### FATS
**Primary digestion location:** small intestine.

---

Fats help our bodies to regulate hormones, help to insulate the body to keep us toasty warm, give us shiny hair and glowing skin ... among a million other cool things. Contrary to the low-fat diet dogma, eating fat does not make you fat – *eye roll*. If that were true, I would be an avocado. Fats are necessary for us to absorb certain vitamins and work wonders for our satiety. Some fats are more awesome than others. Oily fish, avocados, olive oil, nuts and seeds are fab natural sources.

MEAL PREP 101

# Build your meals like a boss

Now you know WHY we need balanced meals, here's how to build them.

**1** CHOOSE A FRESH BASE
Such as salad greens or vegies

→ **2** CHOOSE A PROTEIN
Think tuna, chicken, eggs or tofu

→ **3** ADD COMPLEX CARBOHYDRATE
Pumpkin, sweet potato and wholegrains all count

**4** ADD SOME HEALTHY FAT
Avocado, nuts, seeds

→ **5** DRIZZLE WITH DELICIOUS DRESSING
(see pages 122–3) or just use plain olive oil

→ **6** ADD SOME FLAVOUR BOMBS
I love herbs and chilli (or see pages 20–23 for other ideas)

= *Boss meal*

MEAL PREP 101

# Flavour bombs

I buy copious amounts of these staples to add epic flavour intensity to any dish. I call them 'flavour bombs'... just a small amount goes a long way and can take a meal from drab to fab in seconds.

| | DESCRIPTION | NOTES |
|---|---|---|
| **Salt** | Salt isn't actually a flavour, but a flavour enhancer. Just a pinch reduces bitterness and increases sweet, sour and umami. Salt gets a bad rap because it can contribute to high blood pressure, but our bodies do need some for electrolyte balance. | Pink salt is particularly grand, because it contains many beneficial minerals. I'm known to eat pink salt flakes direct from the pinch-pot, so maybe don't follow my lead on that one. *Confession* |
| **Black pepper** | I'm actually not a big pepper fan (cringe) but it does have a place in my kitchen. Just a pinch can increase the intensity of flavours. | The potassium in pepper can stimulate digestion and discourage bloating. |
| **Chilli, fresh or dried** | A little goes a long way here. Even if you're not big on spicy food, just a pinch can boost the flavour of a meal tenfold. | Chilli can suppress appetite and relieve muscle aches and cramps. |
| **Miso** | This salty fermented soybean paste adds delicious umami flavour to any dish. Don't be afraid to add it to sweet things too, for balance. Check out the Banana PB and miso smoothie on page 184. | Miso contains beneficial bacteria, just like yoghurt and kombucha! |
| **Garlic** | This traditional aromatic is used as a base for many flavoursome dishes. Think dips, pasta sauces, stir-fries. It is thought to help lower blood pressure. | Fresh is best, but I'll turn a blind eye if you want to use the crushed stuff from a jar, or even dried flakes. I think that grating garlic is a total pain in the arse. |

| | DESCRIPTION | NOTES |
|---|---|---|
| **Spring onions** | Sometimes called scallions in the USA and shallots in Australia, these are the long green onions with a white tip. | Thinly slice and refrigerate in a glass container, ready to scatter over salads, meat and fish. |
| **Cinnamon** | Famous for its sweet profile, cinnamon is totally underrated in savoury dishes. Add it to foods that are high in natural sugar (such as bananas or dates) to help reduce the immediate impact on your blood-sugar levels. | Cinnamon has the highest antioxidant value of any spice. *Clever stuff* |
| **Coriander** | These fragrant, citrusy leaves are awesome toppers to almost any savoury dish. Mix into salads, mash into avocado or scatter over dinner. Coriander is an antioxidant powerhouse that helps improve digestion. | I once heard on a breakfast TV show that we are born with tastebuds that either love or hate coriander, depending on genetics. I used to pick it out of every meal, and now I LOVE it, so I think I've funked that theory. |
| **Citrus** | Lemons, limes, oranges and grapefruits are delicious in salad dressing, and add acidity and tangy flavour. | These guys are a great source of vitamin C to strengthen the immune system and help keep skin smooth. |
| **Paprika** | A spice made from ground capsicums (bell peppers). | Sweet and smoked paprika varieties are available, and both add delicious earthy flavours to food. |
| **Sriracha** | A type of hot sauce that originated in Thailand. I love it because it usually has very minimal added sugar (be sure to check the label, though). | Great for adding heat to dressings, meat and everything in between. |
| **Capers** | These delicious little green balls are actually unripened flower buds, pickled in brine or dried. | They add a lemony, salty flavour boost to any savoury dish, particularly fish, pasta and sauces. |

MEAL PREP 101

# Simple shortcuts

We're trying to make everything here as efficient as humanly possible. In a perfect world, we'd all have plenty of time to make our own nut milks, salad dressings and fish stock from scratch. Reality check: unless I dedicate a whole day to meal prep, this isn't going to happen. If you need to make shortcuts to save even more time, these are some smart choices.

| | |
|---|---|
| **Grains** | Microwaveable rice or quinoa sachets are fine if you're in a hurry. |
| **Nut milk** | Buy UHT nut milk. Making your own is kind of a bind if you don't have a total love for it. Avoid brands with added carrageen, oils and sugar. |
| **Spice mixes** | These are easy to pick up in most stores. Check the ingredients to ensure there's no added sugar: it's lurking everywhere. |
| **Sauces and dressings** | You can absolutely keep it simple, if making a dressing from scratch is in your too-hard basket. You definitely have the energy to pinch your fingers together and squeeze a wedge of lemon or lime — a great alternative to an elaborate dressing, as is a drizzle of olive or avocado oil. |
| **Trail mix** | Can't be bothered to make your own? WHY ARE YOU EVEN HERE? Jokes. Just make sure there are no added oils or lots of sugar — they're often hiding. |

**Spiralised vegies**

If you haven't jumped on the bandwagon and smugly bought a cheapo spiraliser on the internet, you're allowed to buy ready-made spiralised vegies from the shops. Or, if you DID jump on the bandwagon and then realised that said cheapo spiraliser was totally rubbish because it was so badly made, you're also allowed to buy ready-made spiralised vegies. We've all been there.

I would add that pre-chopped vegies such as pumpkin and broccoli are a good option, but if you really don't have time to push a knife through some veg, you probably don't have time to be reading this book, either.

**Stock**

In all honesty, making my own stock or even just remembering to reserve the cooking liquid is sometimes beyond my capacity. I keep a carton of liquid stock in my cupboard for emergencies. Stock cubes do the trick too. No judgement. Keep your eye on the sodium content though – many are super salty.

**Frozen cooked prawns**

I have a stash of these in my freezer and I ain't ashamed to say it. I can defrost a handful in 10 minutes by sticking them in a colander and running room-temp water over them. When I'm feeling super lazy, they're a tasty lean protein option that requires zero cooking. See page 174 for ways to use them in Combo plates.

**Vegetable rice**

Replacing carb-laden rice with finely chopped vegies such as broccoli and cauliflower adds an extra serve of veg and reduces carbs in one go. Don't have a blender? Just hate washing the veg? That's totally fair. Save yourself 10 minutes and just buy the ready-made stuff.

**Microwave myth buster**

Think microwaves nuke your food? Microwave technology channels radio waves to excite the molecules in the food, causing them to vibrate and build thermal energy (heat). It's true that some nutrients such as vitamin C are affected by heat, however cooking food faster in a microwave can mean less heat exposure than other cooking methods such as boiling. It makes sense, then, that vitamin C and other water-soluble nutrients are actually better preserved when using a microwave to cook food. Who knew?

MEAL PREP 101

# My favourite snacks

Snacks shouldn't be complicated. The simpler the choice (effortless if possible), the more likely you'll make a good one. So stock up your fridge with these grab-and-go goodies.

| | |
|---|---|
| **Boiled eggs** (see page 44) | Also touted as 'nature's multivitamin', eggs make healthy, portable snacks. Boil up a dozen for the week; chop them and throw them on top of salads or just grab and go when hunger hits. Don't forget a sprinkle of salt. |
| **Blueberries + raspberries** | Berries are the perfect snack when you're craving something sweet. While strawbs totally have a place in my heart (and fridge), I want to be able to throw stuff in my mouth without chopping it up or dripping juice down my shirt (which happens most of the time). |
| **Hummus + vegies** (See page 86) | Once your fridge is like a salad bar (we're getting to that: hold tight), you can just grab a handful of fresh vegies and dunk them in hummus for a speedy, nutritious way to fill up. Hummus is packed with fibre that slows the digestion, keeping your tummy from rumbling for a while longer. |
| **Proghurt** | Protein yoghurt: one of the mainstays of my snack cycle because it kicks any sweet cravings and fills me up for hours. If you don't tolerate dairy, look for lactose-free options or go for coconut yoghurt. Prep a family-size tub in advance or just mix as you need: 1 scoop of protein powder (about 25 g or 1 oz) to 180 g (6½ oz) of yoghurt usually does the trick, but you can add more or less if you like. Look for protein powders that are naturally sweetened and minimally processed. |
| **Bliss balls** (See page 146) | Indulge your sweet cravings the healthy way with portable protein balls. Skip the ready-made ones that so often have added preservatives and flavours. I love to batch-make and freeze mine. |
| **Nuts** | Just 30 g (1 oz) of your favourite nuts (or nut butter) makes for an awesome, nutrient-rich snack. |

MEAL PREP 101

# Supermarket saviours

For those days when you get to work and realise you've forgotten your lunch, or you just can't seem to get organised. You don't need to run to the nearest fast-food outlet; your supermarket has some super-handy and healthy goodies to buy on the fly. Get in there and get some.

| | |
|---|---|
| **Protein bars or balls** | Look for low-sugar, natural options with only a handful of ingredients. Most are date-based, so can be on the sugary side. Eat in moderation: some are candy bars in disguise. |
| **Nuts** | Ideally opt for the raw versions: the ingredients list shouldn't contain anything but the nuts and maybe a pinch of salt. |
| **Hard-boiled eggs** | Most supermarkets sell hard-boiled eggs now, so jump on them for a dose of healthy fats and protein. Win! There is a method for boiling a fresh egg in a kettle, but I don't want to make everyone's tea taste like egg. Proceed with caution, or follow the instructions on page 44. |
| **Plain Greek yoghurt** | No sugar or fruit added, please. Go plain (check the ingredients) and add berries or a sachet of stevia from your local café for sweetness, if needed. Another confession: I may or may not swipe a couple of extra sachets of stevia and throw them in my pocket when I'm buying coffee. |
| **Berries** | Great on their own or added to yoghurt and oats. Make sure you wash these properly because they have often been sprayed. |
| **Roast chicken** | At a push, a roast chicken without the stuffing can be a good call. I don't eat the skin, because I don't like the texture. |

**Tinned tuna**

Line-caught is a good option if you can find it. I like to buy mine in spring water or brine and add my own good-quality olive oil as a dressing, so I can control the amount. Tinned smoked oysters are totally underrated: give them a try.

**Jerky**

Look for only meat and spices on the ingredients label, as sugar is often added. Let's be clear: sugar isn't the devil, but it does sneak into a lot of packaged foods.

**Hard tofu**

Another good protein source that doesn't have heaps of additives. Skip the silken version because it's wibbly and will probably drip all over your shirt.

**Hummus + carrots or celery sticks**

Most supermarkets sell pre-cut celery and carrot sticks. Grab some along with a tub of hummus. Hummus should be made with olive oil or no oil. Some brands sneak in less healthy oils, so keep an eye on the ingredients list.

**Salad bags**

Pick up the leaves that are washed and ready to eat. No-one wants to see you DIYing a human salad spinner, twirling around the office with your leaves. (Unless you really don't want to keep your job, that is.)

**Quick oats sachets**

Mix them up in a mug with a bit of boiling water if you don't have access to a microwave. Buy the plain ones. Flavoured versions, like 'creamy honey', have added stuff you just don't need. Throw in some berries for sweetness if you like.

*I love to add a pinch of stevia and cinnamon*

**Tip**

If you're buying ready-made stuff, I recommend that you learn to read food labels and spot the red herrings. Ideally avoid yukky corn oils, thickeners, additives, e-numbers, flavours, or one of the vast array of added sugars that commercial manufacturers add to foods to make them addictive and cheap to produce. If you see an ingredient you don't like, look for alternative products on the shelf. Top tip: ingredients are listed in order of volume.

MEAL PREP 101

# Your fridge as a salad bar

We all love the food-court salad bar: container after container of different pre-cut salad components so you can build your own with all your favourites. You're about to recreate that for yourself at home. Welcome to your new fridge system.

Meal prep is made a thousand times easier if you cut and chop everything and store it in containers ready to grab and go. Not only does it make healthy eating and food assembly that much easier, but it also helps ensure you don't leave stuff in the crisper until it is covered in fridge slime weeks later. It also means you only get your knife and chopping board out once, instead of multiple times during the week. It's honestly a game changer. SO... here's how to turn your fridge into the best-looking salad bar you ever did see.

## 1 Clean out your fridge
Go to your fridge right now (assuming you're at home; don't go poking in other people's) and pull out any rotten fruits and vegies, sauces past their use-by dates, questionable dairy products and other things you're never going to eat. Toss it out.

## 2 Go meal-prep shopping
Restock all your favourite fruits and vegies, but only enough for the next five days or it's getting relegated to the freezer. Flip through this book and, if something takes your fancy, work out what you need to make it and what you already have.

## 3 Prep
As soon as you get home from the shops, you're going to prep. There's no point in squeezing it all haphazardly in the fridge and then pulling it all out again. Get out a chopping board and your favourite sharp knife. Grab your spiraliser too, if you have one. At the same time, grab some storage containers and set them out.

## 4 Chop
* Halve tomatoes
* Cut corn kernels off the cob
* Chop onions
* Cut carrots into sticks
* Wash celery and cut into hand-length batons
* Spiralise zucchini
* Wrap herbs in damp paper towels

And so on and so on. You get the idea.

**Bonus points:** poach chicken breasts (see pages 50–51) and cook grains (see page 89) on the stove while you get on with the chopping. If you have space, you can also prep things like your Perfect roast veg (see page 102), ready to toss onto a tray.

## 5 Store
Pop all your goodies into containers and pack your fridge. Got space for some dressings? Now is a super time to jump on that too. Grab a jar, turn to pages 122–23, throw in the ingredients for the dressing of your choice and shake. Store it in the fridge door. Now you have something resembling an EPIC SALAD BAR, ready to pick and choose.

Want a snack? You'll be more tempted to grab a handful of cherry tomatoes or radishes and hummus if everything's already prepped.

### Time-saving tip

Don't peel fruits and vegies: the skin adds extra crunch and fibre. Just give them a good rinse under the tap. Ignore this tip for bananas: obviously their skin tastes GROSS.

MEAL PREP 101

# Prep your freezer

Your freezer is where you store part-prepped ingredients and leftover meals. Freeze soups, stews and pasta sauces in individual containers, ready for quick midweek meals. You'll find heaps to freeze in Step 2, when you're batch-making like a boss too. Here's what you'll always find in my freezer.

### Cheese
I don't eat heaps of cheese, but the larger blocks are usually more cost-effective. When I know I won't get through a whole block, I freeze half, or whatever is left, to cut down on waste. It will keep well for about two months. It often goes a bit more crumbly, once thawed, but still tastes delish. Tip: grate it before freezing to speed up the thawing time.

### Cream
Again, I don't use heaps of this, so any leftover cream goes into icetrays or freezer-safe jars. Sour cream is the exception: this tends to separate when frozen so use it up or toss it out.

### Nuts + seeds
These guys have a high fat content, so they store super-well in the freezer and will last a year or more. What's best is you can eat them straight from the freezer without defrosting — they're just a bit crunchier, which makes them all the more delicious!

### Frozen vegetables
If you're in a pinch and forgot to buy veg on the way home, freezer veg will always save you. Buy bags of frozen peas, beans, corn kernels, broccoli and cauliflower and keep them in the freezer for emergencies. If you're really on the ball, you can chop and blanch your own fresh vegies and freeze them in airtight containers.

### Frozen berries
Freeze your own when they're fresh and in season and they'll be loaded with nutrients when you come to eat them. Great for crumbles, smoothies, baking, or to throw into some plain yoghurt for a chilled snack on a summer's day.

### Paleo bread (see pages 90–91)
I always slice and freeze any leftovers, ready to whip up a nutritious snack or meal. Defrost it and lightly toast it to bring back its texture and flavour when you're ready to eat it.

### Sliced chicken meatloaf (see pages 52–53)
Ready to toast and serve with a spread of avocado, or toss chunks through a salad.

### Icetrays with random stuff
I fill icetrays with leftover sauces, hummus, the last of my homemade pesto, citrus juice, and chopped herbs with olive oil. You can wrap these to stop other flavours permeating them, or buy trays with lids, if you're super-organised.

### Ginger

Whole pieces of ginger can be tossed in the freezer in a resealable plastic bag or airtight container. When you want to use some, no need to defrost. Just grate straight into your tea, stir-fry or dressing. No more fuzzy fridge ginger!

### Chopped onion and garlic

Whenever I have these guys going to waste, I freeze them. Toss them into your frying pan straight from the freezer to add flavour to so many dishes.

### Smoothie bags (see pages 82–83)

Totally not a new idea, but absolutely worth mentioning as a meal-prep concept. Whenever you have leftover fruits and vegies that have seen better days, chop them up and throw them in a resealable plastic bag. I leave three or four in the freezer and keep adding to them and taking out what I need, when I need it.

### Cooked grains

Cook, let them cool, and store them in an airtight container in the freezer. When you're ready to use them, put them in a bowl and reheat in the microwave or add to a saucepan on the stovetop with a splash of water.

**Freezer tips**

Different zones of your freezer will cool at different rates. When freezing liquid leftovers such as smoothies and soups, put the containers in the coldest part of your freezer (usually the bottom drawer) to increase the speed at which the food is frozen. This prevents the formation of those large ice crystals that give a yucky texture to the defrosted food.

Don't forget that food expands when it freezes, so don't fill containers to the brim. This will avoid messy explosions and broken containers.

MEAL PREP 101

# Storage containers

My top piece of advice here is to use containers that you already have and buy new ones or replacements only when you need them. Make sure you have a range of sizes and that they are stackable for easier storage.

I've tried many containers for storing prepped ingredients and leftovers. Some haven't worked well – they don't stack, or they don't keep things fresh – so they've been relegated to the pantry. I now have a few favourites on rotation in the fridge that get used every week to store lunches, snacks and chopped vegies.

### Glass vs plastic

Glass containers are great for keeping things crispy or hard. If you're storing cookies, for example, glass containers will help them keep their crunch. They're usually easier to clean than plastic, and don't stain. They also work well when reheating food, if that's your thing.

Plastic containers, on the other hand, can be lightweight and easy to stack. Look for the ones that are BPA free. Bonus points if they're also dishwasher and microwave safe.

My personal preference is glass, although it can be heavy to tote to work. Consider whether you commute on foot and are carting your food around – in which case you're going to love lightweight plastic containers.

I also have a few extras in my food storage system: beeswax fabric wraps for smaller items or to replace a missing lid from a glass jar (just add a rubber band); and cotton produce bags, a great solution for loose fruit and veg such as apples, lemons, capsicums etc. They're both reusable and environmentally friendly.

### Leakability (not a real word)

Whether you go for plastic or glass, make sure it has an airtight seal. This will stop it dripping all over your handbag/manbag. (The maker of my favourite pink wallet does NOT know how to get soy sauce off leather – dammit!) If you're clumsy like me, invest in leakproof containers and even a reusable lunch bag.

### Durability

Cheap, thin plastic containers (like the ones you get takeaway food in) are fine in the fridge, but it's unlikely they'll travel well. For grab-and-go food, make sure you have some stronger options on hand. They'll generally last longer, and price-per-use means it works out as a better investment.

### Size

Life can be so much easier if you have a range of sizes: it means you can save everything from a couple of tablespoons of leftover sauce to an entire meal's worth of vegies.

### Recycling

Glass jars are awesome. Next time you finish a jar of olives or honey, clean it well and use it to store snacks, sauces, smoothies, leftover stock, and so on. Jars are durable and FREE! I get a lot of glass containers from second-hand stores and give them a really good clean. Not only are you spending money for a good cause, but you're recycling too. Just be sure to check for any chips or cracks. Clean family-size yoghurt tubs can be reused to make and store overnight oats (page 80) and proghurt (page 26).

**Tip**

Stackable storage containers are space-savers as well as time-savers.

MEAL PREP 101

# Meal prep kitchen equipment

You don't need fancy gadgets to get started on your meal prep. Keep it simple with the essentials when you're starting out. It's likely you'll already have enough of these to get you up and running. That being said, a well-equipped kitchen is super-helpful and will save you even more time.

### Baking paper and foil
Saves things sticking to your pans, and saves washing-up time too.

### Baking trays
I always have three of these on hand at any one time, because my oven is usually multitasking on every shelf.

### Chef's knife
Great for tough vegies: think pumpkin, raw beetroot and sweet potato.

### Chopping board
I have an EXTRA LARGE one so I can chop up heaps of things and pile them up on the same board. Perfect when prepping your fridge as a salad bar, and for everything in between.

### Grater (or food processor with grater attachment)
Grate carrot, cheese and zucchini (if you don't feel like spiralising).

### Icetrays
For freezing cooked mashed vegies, leftover dressings, leftover smoothies and so on.

### Kitchen scissors
Sturdy scissors you'll be using for a million tasks, from trimming up chicken breast to chopping fresh herbs.

### Loaf tin
If you have a silicone one, it's super-handy because you don't have to line it with baking paper, but any non-stick tin will do.

### Measuring jug
To measure out liquids, or for making and storing sauces, ready to pour.

### Mixing bowls
Grab two – a medium and large – so you can prep a few things at the same time without hassle.

### Serrated knife
Slides through soft fruits and vegies with ease: strawberries, tomatoes, etc.

### Silicone spatula
Mix, spread and even turn things while sautéing. This is an awesome multi-use tool.

### Spiraliser
Grab a cheap one if you're feeling lucky, or make an investment in a good one, available in most kitchen equipment shops.

### Tongs
To move, grip and turn food.

### Utility or paring knife
Good for chopping smaller, fiddly things, such as garlic, ginger and chilli.

### Whisk
For adding air to ingredients when mixing them together. Hello light and fluffy!

### Zester
Super-useful when adding citrus peel for flavour in savoury and sweet dishes. If you don't have one, a cheese grater or some fancy knife skills will do the trick just as well.

*Step 1*

# PREP YOUR PROTEIN

STEP 1 PREP YOUR PROTEIN

# Salmon gravlax

**Portions** 10 | **Hands-on prep time** 30 minutes

This no-cook salmon feels like it should be for special occasions only, but it's so simple to make and freezes well too. I love mine with the Oaty seed crackers (see page 96) and fresh goat's cheese.

240 g (¾ cup) rock salt
1 bunch dill, coarsely chopped
zest from 2 organic lemons

1 kg fresh salmon fillet,
or 4 skinless salmon fillets

1. Combine the salt, dill and lemon zest in a bowl.

2. Spread half of the mixture over the base of a glass or ceramic dish and lay the salmon on top.

3. Top with the remaining salt mixture.

4. Cover and refrigerate for 24 hours, turning after 12 hours.

5. Remove the salmon from the dish, wash away any loose salt mixture and pat dry with paper towel.

6. Slice just before eating. Holding a sharp knife at a 45 degree angle, slice the salmon across the grain as thinly as possible.

**Save**

Salt-cured gravlax can be covered and kept in the fridge for up to 12 days. Freeze whole pieces for up to 2 months and defrost before slicing.

STEP 1 PREP YOUR PROTEIN

# Foolproof oven-baked salmon

Portions 4  |  Hands-on prep time 5 minutes

Salmon is so delicious and easy to prep. It's my go-to meal after a long day. You really can't go wrong with this super-simple method for cooking it.

1  Preheat the oven to 180°C.

2  Pat the salmon dry with paper towel and rub with the olive oil.

3  Place the salmon in a roasting tin, skin-side down. Transfer to the oven.

4  Salmon needs to be cooked for around 4–5 minutes per 1.25 cm of thickness. Since most fillets are around 2.5 cm at their thickest part, check for 'doneness' at around the 8-minute mark. Fish is cooked when it can be easily flaked with a fork (without the help of a knife to rip it apart).

5  Serve with a sprinkling of sea salt flakes, freshly ground black pepper and some sprigs of dill or basil, if using.

4 salmon fillets, skin on
2 tablespoons olive oil
2 teaspoons sea salt flakes
Freshly ground black pepper
Dill and basil sprigs, to serve (optional)

That salt + fat combo is SO GOOD

**Save**

Keep leftover fillets refrigerated for up to 5 days. They can be gently reheated or eaten cold.

**Tip**

I totally urge you to try salmon medium–rare. My mum crucified it for years, not knowing that you can eat good-quality salmon totally raw. Now I'm the biggest lover of the flavourful, super-soft pink flesh in the middle: a much more delicious mouth feel and the flavour is more delicate.

### Sugar-free teriyaki glaze

Mix together 3 tablespoons soy sauce or tamari + 2 teaspoons sesame oil + 1 teaspoon freshly grated ginger + 1 tablespoon dijon mustard + 10 drops liquid stevia. Before baking, baste the salmon and sprinkle with 1 tablespoon of sesame seeds.

# Meal-prepped eggs 101

These nutrition powerhouses are great ready-to-eat snacks, and delicious added to a vegie dish for a protein boost. You can cook them in advance and store them in the fridge. WINNING!

### Boiled

Everyone has their own way of boiling eggs. Some begin with a pan of cold water, but I'm all about speed when it comes to meal prep. If you're anything like me, you love your whites set but your yolk gooey. For convenience sake, I don't want to bite into an egg and have yolk running down my face (that has TOTALLY happened to me) so I've perfected the gooey yolk without the drip factor.

Put water in a saucepan and bring to a simmer. Reduce heat to medium, then lower in eggs (gently, no cracked shells if poss!) and immediately set the timer on your phone for 6 minutes. When the time is up, tip out the hot water and run cold water over the eggs for a few minutes to stop them cooking further. Allow to cool completely before storing them in a bowl in the fridge – or back in the carton. Be sure to write 'BOILED' on the carton to avoid eggcidents.

4 minutes – very runny
6 minutes – gooey
8 minutes – stodgy
10 minutes – hard-boiled

*Good for slicing and grating over stuff*

4 mins · 6 mins · 8 mins · 10 mins

### Tip

Fresher eggs are harder to peel, so use older eggs for boiling. Only peel boiled eggs when you're ready to eat them – they will keep for longer with the shells on.

### Poached

You can prep your favourite poachies up to 5 days before eating, and store them in the fridge.

To start, break a very fresh egg into a sieve and swirl it a little to remove any watery white, then pop it into a bowl. This stops the whites from doing that foamy thing all over your pan. Repeat with up to five more eggs (this will work with a medium-to-large pan: do a few less if you only have a small one).

Tip the eggs slowly into a pan of simmering water, ideally one at a time. Don't worry – as long as the yolks haven't broken, they won't stick together into one very large egg (though, that could be kinda awesome). When they've been in the hot water for around 15 seconds, stir gently to distribute the eggs around the pan. After 3–4 minutes the egg whites will be set and the yolks still gooey. Using a slotted spoon, carefully remove the eggs one by one, and pop them into container filled with cold water – a few ice cubes can help stop the cooking process.

To reheat the eggs without overcooking them, fill a bowl with hot water (from your tap, not boiling) and lower in the eggs you're about to serve. Leave them to warm up for 2 minutes, then remove with a slotted spoon and serve.

*A one-quart mason jar is the perfect size to hold a dozen eggs*

### Pickled

Okay, you might associate pickled eggs with pub food or fish-and-chip shops, but they are delicious and an awesome way of making something nutritious and versatile in batches. Plus they keep in the fridge for AGES. In other words, these bad boys are meal-prep VIPs.

The more you can pickle at once, the less time spent cooking in the future. I recommend doing a full dozen and getting your hands on a huge jar for this one.

To make pickled eggs, boil the eggs in the shell for a full 10 minutes. When they are cool, peel off the shells.

In a saucepan over medium-high heat, bring all of the remaining ingredients to the boil, then reduce the heat and simmer for 5 minutes.

Remove from the heat and allow the vinegar mixture to cool slightly. Put the eggs into a sterilised jar and pour the vinegar mixture over the top until the jar is full and all the eggs are completely covered. Allow to cool completely before putting on the lid and refrigerating for up to 4 months.

You can enjoy these just a few days after pickling, but they taste EXTRA after a week or two.

### Ingredients

12 eggs
½ teaspoon mustard seeds
375 ml (1½ cups) white or apple cider vinegar
185 ml (¾ cup) water
2 teaspoons sea salt
2 sprigs fresh tarragon
1 garlic clove, quartered

*Love garlic? Add a few extra cloves*

**Save**

These last 3–4 months in the fridge.

STEP 1 PREP YOUR PROTEIN

# One-tray chicken: three ways

Portions 6  |  Hands-on prep time 10 minutes

When you're rotating lean meats such as chicken for a lot of meals, dinner can get pretty tedious. This simple hack lets you cook chicken three different ways in one tray. I'm so keen on multitasking! Use foil to pinch up dividing walls in your pan so you can season each portion differently. Use your fave seasonings or try mine.

3 large skinless chicken breasts
2 tablespoons olive oil
1 teaspoon each salt + pepper

1 tablespoon each of seasonings, opposite

1   Preheat the oven to 180°C.

2   Using a pair of kitchen scissors, trim off any white sinew from the meat, then cut it into 2 cm pieces.

3   Lay an extra-large piece of foil on a baking tray, spread out the chicken and drizzle with olive oil. Season with salt and pepper.

4   Divide the chicken evenly into three portions, and pinch two 'walls' in the foil to create separate sections, as shown.

5   Season each section with a different seasoning mixture, rub into the chicken, and bake for 10–15 minutes or until cooked through.

**Save**

Keep the cooked chicken in separate airtight containers in the fridge for up to 4 days.

48

## My top 3 chicken seasonings

### Spicy barbecue

Smoked paprika + garlic powder + onion powder + chilli powder

### Maple sesame

1 tablespoon maple syrup + 2 tablespoons sesame seeds + 1 teaspoon garlic powder + 1 teaspoon ground ginger

### Lemon + rosemary

Lemon zest + lemon juice + finely chopped fresh rosemary

STEP 1 PREP YOUR PROTEIN

# Milk-poached chicken

**Serves** 4 | **Hands-on prep time** 10 minutes

Poached chicken offers a deliciously consistent moist texture, and takes less time than you'd think. The milk captures the flavours and can be reserved and used as a soup base (see opposite).

750 ml (3 cups) milk (I use unsweetened almond milk)
4 garlic cloves or 2 teaspoons garlic powder
10 peppercorns
Fresh tarragon (optional)
4 skinless, boneless chicken breasts

1. Heat the milk in a saucepan over medium heat, together with the garlic, peppercorns and tarragon (if using), until just simmering.

2. Lower the chicken breasts into the poaching liquid and set a timer for 15–20 minutes, depending on their size.

3. Remove the chicken from the poaching liquid and set aside.

4. Allow to cool before slicing or shredding the chicken into long strands with your hands.

**Save**
Store in an airtight container in the fridge for up to 4 days.

**Tip**
You can poach chicken in the same amount of stock, or plain old water, if you're trying to keep it super simple. Same method and cooking times apply.

*(+ soup with the leftovers)*

### Soup

Reserve the poaching liquid for soup: throw in 1½ cups of your oldest vegies (I usually have extra celery and leek) and simmer for 15 minutes. If you want extra flavour, add a chicken stock cube. Blend until smooth, with a good dollop of mustard if you like. Cool and store in the fridge; it will be good for 2–3 days. You can freeze it in single-serve portions too.

STEP 1 PREP YOUR PROTEIN

# Basic chicken meatloaf  *Slice + freeze*

**Portions** 8 | **Hands-on prep time** 10 minutes

Slice meatloaf into single-serve portions before freezing and defrost at room temp whenever you want a satisfying protein punch.

1. Preheat the oven to 180°C.

2. Put all of the ingredients into a bowl and use your hands to mix until well combined.

3. Press the mixture into a silicone loaf tin (or a loaf tin lined with baking paper) and bake for 40–45 minutes until cooked through. Set aside for 10 minutes before removing from the tin and slicing.

4. You can also spoon the mixture into the holes of a muffin tin to cook individual portions.

500 g chicken mince
1½ cups grated vegetables*
4 eggs
3 tablespoons Caramelised onions (see page 104) or 1 medium onion, chopped
1½ teaspoons finely chopped garlic (or 1 teaspoon garlic powder)
1 tablespoon Worcestershire sauce (see opposite for flavour bomb substitutions)
½ teaspoon sea salt flakes
Freshly ground black pepper

*\* I love zucchini and carrot*

**Save**

Freeze the slices between sheets of baking paper for up to 1 month. Store in an airtight container in the fridge for up to 4 days.

### Flavour bombs

Replace Worcestershire sauce with any one of these options:

* chopped fresh coriander
* 1 tablespoon mustard
* 1 tablespoon chilli flakes
* 1 tablespoon miso paste
* 1 tablespoon sriracha

STEP 1 PREP YOUR PROTEIN

# Nut butter falafel

Makes about 18  |  Hands-on prep time 20 minutes

Chickpeas and nut butter are great vegetarian protein options. Add your favourite flavour combo from the options below or invent your own.

1. Preheat the oven to 180°C.
2. Mix all of the ingredients together in a blender or food processor until they are well combined.
3. Add your choice of flavours to the mixture in the blender (see below for some suggestions).
4. Roll the mixture into balls with your hands. If the dough is a little wet, add more almond meal or flour, a little at a time.
5. Place the balls on a silicone baking sheet or a baking tray lined with baking paper. Bake for 20 minutes or until golden brown.

400 g tin chickpeas, drained and rinsed
½ cup chopped cooked pumpkin (see page 100)
50 g (½ cup) almond meal or other flour
1 teaspoon baking powder
3 tablespoons natural peanut butter
1 tablespoon lemon juice

*Almond butter and tahini also work - whatever you have in the cupboard is fine*

**Save**
Store in the fridge for 5 days, or freeze for up to 2 weeks.

*My top 3 flavour combos*

**Traditional**
2 teaspoons cumin
+ 1 teaspoon allspice
+ 1 teaspoon onion powder

**Moroccan**
2 teaspoons turmeric
+ 1 teaspoon garam masala + 1 teaspoon garlic powder

**Green goodness**
½ bunch fresh basil
+ ½ bunch fresh mint
+ 2 tablespoons pine nuts

STEP 1 PREP YOUR PROTEIN

# Cauliflower steaks

Portions 4   |   **Hands-on prep time** 10 minutes

Slice a cauliflower into thick 'steaks'. Save any rogue florets to make vegetable rice, or toss them into smoothie bags (see pages 82–83).

1. Preheat the oven to 180°C.

2. Remove the large outer leaves from the cauliflower (leaving some on is fine) and trim the stalk.

3. Slice lengthways through the centre to produce four 2 cm–thick 'steaks'.

4. Lay the steaks on a baking tray lined with baking paper. Drizzle with olive oil and flip over to coat both sides.

5. Sprinkle with salt, pepper and any herbs or spices that take your fancy.

6. Roast for 25–30 minutes until golden and tender.

**1 large cauliflower**
**Olive oil**
**1 tablespoon of your favourite herb or spice mixture**

**Make**

Make these at the same time as your Perfect roast veg (see page 102)

**Save**

Store in the fridge, covered, for up to 3 days.

**Tip**

These work well as a toast substitute for brekkie. Top with sliced avocado and a poached egg (see page 45) for a super-quick nutritious start to the day.

### Indian twist

Add curry powder and garam masala before roasting, and serve with plain yoghurt, a handful of raisins and some fresh coriander for a delicious vegie dish!

STEP 1 PREP YOUR PROTEIN

# Miso eggplant

Portions 4  |  Hands-on prep time 10 minutes

Add a little Japanese flavour to your busy weekdays with this simple miso eggplant. While eggplant isn't technically a protein, it's often the star of a vegetarian dinner plate.

2 eggplants
Olive oil cooking spray
1 tablespoon miso paste
1½ tablespoons soy sauce or tamari
3 cm piece of fresh ginger, grated
2 large garlic cloves, finely chopped
1 teaspoon coconut sugar
Black sesame seeds, to serve

1   Preheat the oven to 180°C.

2   Using a sharp knife, cut the eggplants lengthways down the middle.

3   Now score the eggplant diagonally one way then the other to create a crosshatch effect. Spray or drizzle with a little olive oil and bake for 20 minutes.

4   Meanwhile, create the glaze by mixing the miso paste with tamari, ginger, garlic, coconut sugar and 60 ml (¼ cup) of water in a small saucepan over high heat.

5   Boil the miso mixture until thickened and brush it over the flesh of the eggplant. Bake for a further 5–10 minutes until caramelised, then remove from the oven. Allow to cool for 5 minutes before serving, sprinkled with the sesame seeds.

Save
Unused portions can be stored in the fridge for up to 3 days.

STEP 1 PREP YOUR PROTEIN

# Lemon-grilled fish

Portions 4  |  Hands-on prep time 10 minutes

This recipe works well with any white-fleshed fish. Try it with mahimahi, basa, barramundi, tilapia or whatever is on special at the fishmonger. It makes an awesome addition to salad or tacos.

1. Preheat the grill on high.

2. Lay the fish in a glass dish or on a baking tray lined with baking paper and drizzle with olive oil.

3. Grate the zest from the lemon and sprinkle it over the fish, then squeeze half the lemon juice over and sprinkle with garlic powder. Thinly slice the remaining lemon half and lay over the top of the fish.

4. Scatter the spring onion and parsley (if using) over the top.

5. Grill for 15-20 minutes until the fish is cooked through and flakes with a fork. Serve scattered with herbs.

4 white-fleshed fish fillets (approximately 200 g each) or 1 whole fish (approximately 1 kg)
2 tablespoons olive oil
1 large lemon
1 teaspoon garlic powder
¼ cup sliced spring onion (scallion)
2 tablespoons chopped fresh parsley (optional)
Fresh herbs, to serve

**Make**

Before cooking, prep the fish and freeze in portions. You can defrost a portion in the fridge before grilling.

**Save**

Cooked fish can be stored in the freezer for up to a month. Store leftovers in the refrigerator overnight.

**Tip**

Many lemons from the supermarket are waxed. Avoid getting wax all over your fish by pouring boiling water from the kettle over the lemon in your kitchen sink. Give it a quick scrub with a vegie brush to remove any residue.

STEP 1 PREP YOUR PROTEIN

# Healthy fish cakes

Portions 4 | Hands-on prep time 15 minutes

These fish cakes can be made kid-friendly by shaping them into fingers and coating with rice flour instead of sesame seeds. Use the same weight of tinned tuna or salmon if you don't have fresh fish.

1 Preheat the oven to 180°C.

2 Throw the whole lot (aside from the sesame seeds) into a blender or food processor and blitz to a coarse consistency.

3 Use wet hands to roll the mixture into patties, then dip into the sesame seeds to coat.

4 Bake for 15-20 minutes until cooked through, or pan-fry in a little oil (sesame oil is YUM) for 3–4 minutes on each side.

500 g fresh white-fleshed fish, coarsely chopped
1 small onion, chopped
1 garlic clove (or ½ teaspoon garlic powder)
½ bunch fresh parsley (stalks and all!)
Juice of ½ lemon
Sea salt + pepper
75 g (½ cup) sesame seeds
Sesame oil, for frying (optional)

*I love these served with salad and Coconut tzatziki (see page 123)*

**Save**
Freeze uncooked patties, before dipping them in the sesame seeds, in an airtight container for up to 3 months.

**Tip**
If you don't have a food processor, just chop everything up reaaaaally finely.

### Make them Thai-style

* 1 cm piece of fresh ginger, grated, or 1 teaspoon ground ginger
* use lime instead of lemon
* use coriander instead of parsley
* 1 tablespoon soy sauce or tamari

STEP 1 PREP YOUR PROTEIN

# Satay tofu crumble

Portions 4  |  Hands-on prep time 10 minutes

Tofu gets a bad rap for being bland, but pump up the flavour and it's something to daydream about (don't pretend you don't think about dinner at work). This version is 10 out of 10 on the flavour scale.

1. Cut tofu into 1 cm thick slices and lay them in a single layer on a plate lined with paper towel. Cover with more paper towel and press down firmly to squeeze out any excess liquid.

2. Heat 1 tablespoon of sesame oil in a large frying pan. Cook the tofu slices for 7–10 minutes until browned on both sides. Transfer to a plate to cool.

3. Meanwhile, whisk together the soy sauce, lime juice, sriracha, peanut butter, ginger and remaining sesame oil in a medium bowl.

4. Crumble the tofu into small pieces and add to the bowl with the sauce. Toss to combine.

500 g firm tofu
2 tablespoons sesame oil
3 tablespoons soy sauce or tamari
2 tablespoons lime juice
1 tablespoon sriracha
5 teaspoons natural crunchy peanut butter
1 teaspoon freshly grated ginger (or ground equivalent)
Basil leaves and crushed peanuts, to serve

**Save**

Satay tofu crumble can be kept, covered, in the fridge for up to 5 days.

STEP 1 PREP YOUR PROTEIN

# Smoky turkey rissoles

**Portions** 3-4  |  **Hands-on prep time** 15 minutes

Enjoy three of these rissoles as part of a main meal, or snack on a couple for a protein kick any time of day.

1. Preheat the oven to 180°C.

2. Put the turkey, spices and salt in a bowl and use your hands to combine well.

3. Grab a palm-sized amount of mixture and roll it into a ball. Press lightly into patties, if you prefer.

4. Place on a baking tray lined with baking paper and repeat with the remaining mixture to make about 9 balls or patties.

5. Bake for 15–20 minutes until beginning to brown on top.

6. Remove from the oven and allow to cool. Serve with micro herbs and extra chilli flakes, if you like.

500 g turkey mince
1 teaspoon garlic powder
1 teaspoon smoked paprika
1 teaspoon chilli flakes (optional)
1 teaspoon sea salt flakes (use smoked salt if you have it!)
Micro herbs and extra chilli flakes, to serve (optional)

*Dunk in green dressing (see page 123)*

**Save**

Store in the fridge for up to 4 days, or freeze for up to 2 months.

**STEP 1 PREP YOUR PROTEIN**

# Asian-style turkey mince

**Portions** 4 | **Hands-on prep time** 5 minutes

This spicy dish is super-versatile for midweek meals and freezes really well. Always defrost and reheat on the same day, making sure it's piping hot.

1. Heat the peanut oil in a frying pan over medium–high heat.
2. Add the turkey mince, garlic and chilli, cooking for 4–5 minutes, stirring regularly, until cooked through.
3. Add the soy, lime and stevia or honey in the final minute of cooking. Stir well to coat the meat, then remove from the heat.
4. Scatter with coriander and fresh chilli. Serve with lime wedges, if you like.

2 tablespoons peanut oil
500 lean turkey mince
2 garlic cloves, crushed, or 1 teaspoon garlic powder
1 red chilli, thinly sliced, or 1 tablespoon dried chilli flakes
3 tablespoons soy sauce or tamari
Zest and juice of 1 lime
½ tablespoon granulated stevia or 1 tablespoon honey
Fresh coriander, sliced red chilli and lime wedges, to serve (optional)

**Save**

Allow cooked mince to cool before storing in an airtight container in the fridge for 3–4 days, or for 2 months in the freezer.

STEP 1 PREP YOUR PROTEIN

# Spicy beef mince

**Portions** 4  |  **Hands-on prep time** 10 minutes

Beef is a lean meat with a high iron and zinc content. Feeling adventurous? Try it with kangaroo mince.

1. Heat the oil in a frying pan over medium heat. Add the garlic, cooking for 1 minute.

2. Add the beef and spring onion, chilli flakes, cumin and cayenne. Mix well and cook for 5 minutes, stirring regularly, until cooked through.

3. Serve with coriander leaves and extra spring onion.

½ tablespoon olive oil or coconut oil
2 garlic cloves, finely chopped
500 g 5% fat beef mince
½ cup chopped spring onion, plus extra to serve
1 tablespoon chilli flakes
1 teaspoon ground cumin
1 teaspoon cayenne pepper
Fresh coriander leaves, to serve

*I keep chopped spring onion in a container in the fridge, ready to scatter over dishes like this*

**Save**

Allow cooked mince to cool before storing in an airtight container in the fridge for 3–4 days, or for 2 months in the freezer.

STEP 1 PREP YOUR PROTEIN

# Chicken crust meatza

Portions 4 | Hands-on prep time 15 minutes

This pizza is great for gluten-free, paleo and keto diets. I love a few slices with a big salad.

1. Preheat a grill on high.

2. Put the chicken, flour, nutritional yeast (if using), garlic, onion and salt in a large bowl. Mix well (I just repeatedly squeeze it between my hands) and spread on a baking tray lined with baking paper. Loosely squish so you can lay another piece of baking paper over the top.

3. Use a rolling pin (or the roll of baking paper with elastic bands or hair ties on the ends to stop it unravelling) to roll out the mixture to about 5 mm thick. Shape it into a rectangle for easier freezing.

4. Peel back the top layer of baking paper and grill for 10–12 minutes until the meat is cooked through and starting to brown on the edges.

5. Remove from under the grill and spread with the passata or pesto. Add toppings (see below), then return to the grill for 5–10 minutes until the toppings are warm and cheese has melted.

6. Remove from the grill and slice to serve. Leftover topped slices can be kept in the fridge for up to 3 days.

500 g lean chicken mince
2 tablespoons coconut flour
¼ cup nutritional yeast (optional)
1 teaspoon garlic powder
1 teaspoon onion powder
1 teaspoon sea salt
125 ml (½ cup) tomato passata (puréed tomato) or pesto

*Enjoy leftovers cold! There's nothing like cold meatza for breakfast.*

**Make**

Topping ideas:
Perfect roast veg (see page 102)
Sliced tomato
Anchovies
Sliced onion
Cheese: mozzarella, cheddar, feta

**Save**

Double this recipe and, after the extra base is grilled, cover and freeze it (without toppings) for up to 2 months. You can pull it out, dress it, and bake for around 25 minutes at 180°C.

**Tip**

I did half-and-half with my toppings. Great option if you're trying to appeal to many tastes! You can sub turkey for the chicken mince, if preferred.

STEP 1 PREP YOUR PROTEIN

# Sweet potatoes with baked eggs

**Portions** 4 | **Hands-on prep time** 15 minutes

You've probably seen eggs baked in avo ALL over Instagram (are you following @sallyoneil?). It's a legit delicious snack. This version is all about healthy complex carbs to keep you fuelled through the day.

1. Preheat the oven to 180°C. Wash the sweet potatoes and stab them all over with a fork.

2. Microwave for 7–8 minutes. If you prefer, you can bake them (but think of the time you'll save!).

3. Cut the cooked potatoes in half, and scoop out about a third of the soft flesh from the centre. Reserve the cooked potato to stir into your overnight oats (see page 80), or mash with miso and serve with fish.

4. Place the halves cut-side up on a baking tray lined with baking paper. Divide the chopped spinach between the potato halves and crack an egg into each one.

5. Bake for 8–12 minutes, depending on how you like your eggs.

2 large sweet potatoes
½ cup chopped spinach
4 eggs
Julienned radish and freshly ground black pepper, to serve (optional)

*Try chopped onion or capsicum instead of spinach*

**Save**

Store the baked potatoes in an airtight container in the fridge for up to 2 days. If you want to store them for longer, make the potatoes up to Step 3 and store in the fridge for up to 4 days.

**Tip**

Get creative with toppings! I love spring onion, radish and black pepper, plus any dressing I have lying around. You should have plenty now you've made up the delish ones from pages 122–23.

*Step 2*

# BATCH AND STASH

STEP 2 **BATCH AND STASH**

# DIY muesli

*Prep two jars of this at a time to last you several weeks!*

---

**GRAINS** (5 cups total, any combination)

Rye flakes · Rolled oats · Barley flakes

**+**

**YOUR CHOICE OF CHOPPED NUTS** (1 cup total)

Brazil nuts · Almonds · Walnuts · Cashews · Peanuts

**+**

**EXTRA CRUNCH FACTOR** (1 cup total)

Sunflower seeds · Pumpkin seeds · Buckwheat groats · Coconut flakes · Cacao nibs · Freeze-dried banana

**+**

**DRIED FRUIT** (½ cup, optional)

Raisins · Goji berries · Blueberries · Mulberries · Raspberries

**+**

**FLAVOUR BOMBS** (½ teaspoon)

Ground cardamom · Ground cinnamon · Sea salt · Ground vanilla

*= quickest breakfast ever!*

## How to eat muesli

### Soak
Add 1 cup milk and leave for a few hours. Kinda like Overnight oats (see page 80).

### Heat
Put ¾ cup muesli and 125 ml (½ cup) milk in a small saucepan and cook for 10 minutes over medium heat, stirring regularly.

### Toast
Add 3 tablespoons honey or your favourite sweetener and 2 tablespoons melted coconut oil to the mix before adding any dried fruit. Stir to coat and spread onto a lined baking tray. Toast in a preheated oven at 180°C for 15–20 minutes until golden brown. Allow to cool and stir in the fruit.

### Top
Scatter muesli over plain Greek yoghurt and add fresh berries for a simple and tasty brekkie.

STEP 2 BATCH AND STASH

# Five days of overnight oats

Portions 5 | Hands-on prep time 10 minutes

Prepping oats in big batches ready for the week ahead is a sure-fire way of saving yourself from the bagel cart at work. The fibre takes a while to digest, so these keep you full for longer (use rolled oats rather than quick ones as they take longer for your body to break down). Not a whiz in the kitchen? If I was to offer one recipe to someone with zero cooking ability who was trying to eat healthily, this would be it. Ten minutes' investment equals a nutritious start to the day for five days. What a pay-off! Do you prefer sweet or savoury?

### Sweet

500 g (5 cups) rolled oats
40 g (¼ cup) chia seeds
1.25 litres (5 cups) milk of your choice
1 teaspoon vanilla extract or ground vanilla

### Savoury

500 g (5 cups) rolled oats
40 g (¼ cup) chia seeds
1.25 litres (5 cups) water, or leftover milk-poached chicken stock (see page 50) or vegetable stock
½ teaspoon sea salt

*Watch out for the high sodium content of some ready-made stock*

Mix all of the ingredients together in a bowl, cover and leave to soak in the fridge. Spoon portions into a small, portable jars or airtight containers and top with your fave topping combos when you're ready to eat them.

### Sweet topping combos

* Walnuts + ½ cup grated carrot + nutmeg + 1 teaspoon honey
* Sliced banana + peanut butter + cinnamon
* Cacao powder + raspberries + toasted coconut + cacao nibs
* DIY trail mix (see page 126) + sliced strawberries + 2 squares dark chocolate

### Savoury topping combos

* Poached egg (see page 45) + avocado + turkey bacon
* ½ teaspoon chilli flakes + 1 teaspoon tamari or soy sauce + coriander + poached chicken (see page 50)
* Tinned sardines + grated zucchini + lemon juice + pepper
* Miso pumpkin mash + chopped Thai basil + cashews

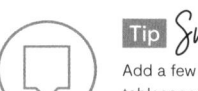

**Tip** *Sweet*
Add a few tablespoons of this to smoothies before blending for extra fibre and creaminess!

**Tip** *Savoury*
Spoon into your soup base before blending to make it thick and super-satisfying.

# DIY smoothie bags

Smoothie bags are a way to save odds and ends of food in the freezer until you're ready to fire up the blender for a delicious and healthy drink. You can chop and freeze any ingredient you might use in a smoothie, using a resealable plastic bag so that you can easily take out as much as you need at a time.

If you want to be a bit more organised, you can portion the ingredients out, ready to blend first thing in the morning so you can run out of the door fast. If you don't have leftovers (who are you?), you can always find some delicious options in the freezer section of the supermarket.

Want to cut the disposable plastic? I use my resealable bags over and over. Give them a wipe with a clean cloth every now and again. Freezer-safe mason jars or containers work too.

### Save

I like to freeze leftover smoothies in icetrays or popsicle moulds. They'll last 3 months in the freezer, so the only thing that might pause your prep is freezer space!

### Tip

Freeze a smoothie in a freezer-safe jar or container. Grab the container as you leave the house in the morning and it will be defrosted in time for lunch; or leave it to defrost in the fridge overnight and have it for your brekkie.

SMOOTHIE BAG

Berries | Coconut chunks | Banana | Mango | Cooked pumpkin | Spinach | Zucchini (leftovers of zoodling) | Broccoli stalks

+

LIQUID (200 ml total)

Milk | Water | Coconut water

+

PROTEIN HIT (30 g)

Scoop of protein powder (optional, but makes it filling)

+

FIBRE

Leafy greens (2 cups) | Oats (1 tablespoon) | Chia | LSA (linseed, sunflower and almond meal) | Psyllium

+

HEALTHY FAT (to taste)

Avocado | Nuts | Seeds | Coconut oil | Nut butter | Coconut yoghurt

= *perfect smoothie every time!*

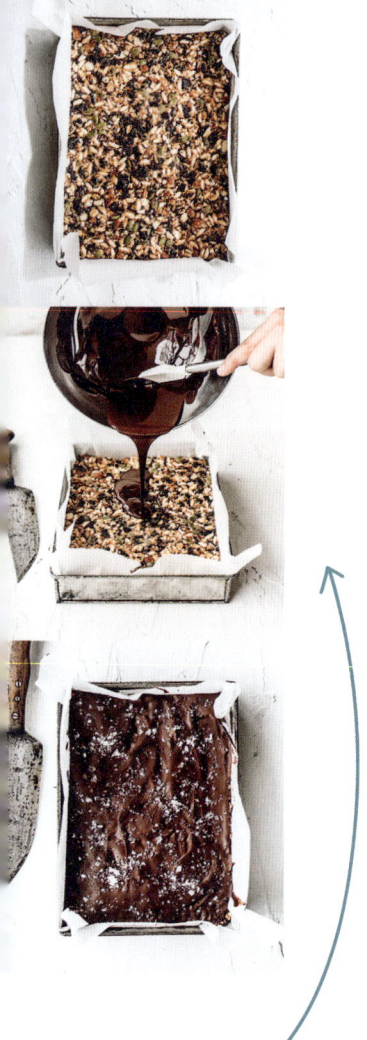

*Enjoy licking this bowl!*

STEP 2 **BATCH AND STASH**

# Smoky chocolate cereal bars

**Portions** 14  |  **Hands-on prep time** 15 minutes

I love a muesli bar as much as the next person, but the ones on supermarket shelves often have a number of suspicious ingredients. Try making a batch of these cereal bars instead. Use plain almonds and salt if you prefer them without the smoky flavour.

2 tablespoons coconut oil
200 g (1 cup) pitted prunes, finely chopped
180 g (⅔ cup) natural peanut or almond butter
1 tablespoon honey or maple syrup
160 g (1 cup) smoked almonds, coarsely chopped
30 g (1 cup) puffed brown rice
30 g (¼ cup) cacao nibs
40 g (¼ cup) pepitas (pumpkin seeds)
150 g dark chocolate (85% cacao), melted
1 teaspoon smoked sea salt

1. Put the coconut oil and prunes in a large wide-based saucepan over low to medium heat and mash with a fork.

2. Stir in the nut butter and honey until well combined and gooey.

3. Remove from the heat and stir through almonds, puffed rice, cacao nibs and pepitas. Mix well.

4. Press the mixture in a layer about 1.5 cm thick into the base of a silicone baking tin or a baking tin lined with baking paper.

5. Pour the melted chocolate over and sprinkle with sea salt.

6. Refrigerate until set (about an hour), then slice into bars.

**Save**

Refrigerate for up to 1 week; freeze for 3 weeks.

STEP 2 BATCH AND STASH

# DIY hummus

**Portions** 10  |  **Hands-on prep time** 10 minutes

Everyone needs a great hummus recipe ... or four. All of the variations here offer a good dose of fibre (which is great for a healthy digestive tract) and pack a punch in the flavour department.

1. Put all of the ingredients into the bowl of a food processor fitted with an S-blade.

2. Process until smooth, stopping to scrape down the sides of the bowl as needed.

- 1 tin of your favourite beans or legumes, drained and rinsed (see options below)
- 1 garlic clove (or ½ teaspoon garlic powder)
- 3 tablespoons olive oil
- 4 tablespoons tahini
- 2 tablespoons lemon juice
- Sea salt + pepper

### My favourite combos

At its heart, hummus is simply beans blended with tahini, olive oil, garlic and lemon. I love these combos.

* lentils + 2 handfuls spinach leaves
* white beans + 1 teaspoon ground cumin
* chickpeas + 1 teaspoon paprika
* black beans + ¼ teaspoon cayenne or chilli

### Save

Store in a glass jar in the fridge for up to 1 week. Freeze in an airtight container (with space at the top to leave room for expansion) for 6 months. Thaw in the refrigerator the day before you want to use it. You can also freeze small portions in an icetray.

# Supergrains

Portions 8 | Hands-on prep time 5 minutes

These grains add new and interesting flavours to any meal, and are less refined than standard white rice. They come with their natural bran and germ, offering you a complete package of nutrition.

1. Put 1 cup of your choice of dry grains (brown rice, buckwheat, teff, freekeh, quinoa or kamut) in a saucepan and cover with 1 litre (4 cups) of water or stock. A pinch of salt is optional. Bring to a boil, then reduce the heat to low, stirring occasionally until the liquid is almost all absorbed and the grain is tender. See right for approximate cooking times.

2. Use a fine sieve for draining so that small grains don't fall through the holes. Set aside to cool before transferring the cooked grains to an airtight container.

### Growing grains

1 cup BROWN RICE
+ 50 minutes cooking time
= 2 cups cooked

1 cup BUCKWHEAT
+ 20 minutes cooking time
= 2 cups cooked

1 cup TEFF
+ 20 minutes cooking time
= 3 cups cooked

1 cup FREEKEH
+ 15 minutes cooking time
= 3 cups cooked

1 cup QUINOA
+ 20 minutes cooking time
= 2 cups cooked

1 cup KAMUT
+ 1 hour 30 minutes cooking time
= 3 cups cooked

*Quinoa*

**Make**
Freeze cooked grains in portions in resealable bags: when you need them for a meal, empty the grains into a bowl of warm water for 15 minutes to defrost, or put them on the stovetop with a splash of water to heat through.

**Save**
Cooked grains will last 3-4 days the fridge, or 2 months in the freezer.

**Tip**
Teff doesn't freeze well, so cook that one as you need it.

*I eat mine with a smear of goat's cheese, drizzled with olive oil and balsamic glaze*

*Olive + oregano*

# One-bowl nutty paleo bread

**Makes** 3 loaves | **Hands-on prep time** 20 minutes

You probably don't want to make bread all that often, because it's a laborious process. It's SO much faster to walk to the corner store – I get it. This recipe is nutritious and unlike any other bread you've tasted, so it's worth the effort. It also makes enough for three loaves, so you only have to measure and mix once every few months. YAY!

Mix together the dry ingredients, right, and store them in an airtight container in your pantry for when that bread craving hits. Feel free to experiment with your own flavour combos: you could even try something a little sweet!

### Dry ingredients

360 g (3 cups) golden linseed (flaxseed) meal
170 g (1½ cups) almond meal
120 g (1 cup) coconut flour
6 tablespoons baking powder
210 g (1½ cups) hazelnuts
220 g (1½ cups) sesame seeds
220 g (1½ cups) sunflower seeds
3 teaspoons sea salt

*Rosemary + garlic*

*Pesto swirl*

1. Pick out a flavour variation below. Preheat the oven to 180°C.

2. Weigh out one-third of the dry ingredients mixture and put it into a bowl, along with your flavour choice. Make a well in the centre and crack in 5 eggs. Add 3 tablespoons liquid coconut oil (not hot, or it will scramble the eggs) and mix well. Spoon the batter into a silicone loaf tin (or a loaf tin lined with baking paper) and bake for 40–45 minutes, until a knife inserted in the centre comes out clean.

3. Allow the bread to cool before removing it from the tin and storing or slicing.

**Save**

Store bread in an airtight container for up to 5 days. Slice before freezing for 4 months: pop a frozen slice in the toaster for quick and easy toast!

## Flavour variations

**Olive + oregano**

+ 60 g (½ cup) pitted olives + 1 tablespoon dried oregano

**Rosemary + garlic**

+ 1 tablespoon chopped fresh rosemary leaves + 2 teaspoons garlic powder

**Pesto swirl**

+ 3 tablespoons pesto (ready-made is fine) or make your own (see page 122) and swirl through the mixture in the loaf tin before baking

STEP 2 **BATCH AND STASH**

# Flax waffles

Portions 8  |  Hands-on prep time 10 minutes

Do you prefer sweet or savoury waffles? This mixture has you covered for both. You can even split the batter and make half and half.

1  Heat a waffle iron.

2  Put the eggs and oil into a blender with 125 ml (½ cup) of water, blending until foamy.

3  Pour the liquid into a bowl containing the linseed meal, baking powder and salt.

4  Fold the mixture together and leave it in the bowl for 3 minutes.

5  Add herbs or cinnamon.

6  Spoon the mixture onto the hot waffle iron, cook and repeat until you have cooked all of the mixture.

5 large eggs
80 ml (⅓ cup) extra virgin olive oil or melted coconut oil
240 g (2 cups) golden linseed (flaxseed) meal
1 tablespoon baking powder
1 teaspoon sea salt
1 tablespoon dried herbs (for savoury waffles) or 2 teaspoons ground cinnamon (for sweet)

**Save**
Freeze cooked waffles between sheets of baking paper in an airtight container for up to 6 weeks. Pop straight into the toaster to defrost.

STEP 2 **BATCH AND STASH**

# Rosemary and tahini cookies

**Portions** 12  |  **Hands-on prep time** 10 minutes

Savoury cookies? I promise you won't be disappointed! If there was only one recipe in this book I would urge everyone to try, it would be this one.

1. Preheat the oven to 160°C. Line a baking tray with baking paper and set aside.

2. Put the tahini and maple syrup into a small saucepan over low heat and melt them together. Add 1 teaspoon of the salt and stir well, then remove from the heat.

3. Mix the almond meal with 1 tablespoon of rosemary in a bowl and stir the hot tahini mixture through.

4. Roll the mixture into 12 balls and set them out on the baking tray. Press the balls down with the back of a fork and sprinkle with the pistachios, remaining rosemary and salt.

5. Bake for 10–12 minutes. Remove from the oven and transfer to a wire rack to cool before storing.

270 g (1 cup) tahini (I used black)
2 tablespoons maple syrup
2 teaspoons sea salt
125 g (1¼ cups) almond meal
2 tablespoons chopped fresh rosemary
1 tablespoon chopped pistachios

**Save**

Store in an airtight container at room temperature for up to 1 week. Freeze for up to 1 month.

STEP 2 **BATCH AND STASH**

# Oaty seed crackers

Makes 30   |   Hands-on prep time 20 minutes

Creating a balanced meal is as much about texture as it is flavour balance and those all-important proteins, fats and carbs. These delicious oaty crackers will add crunch to any meal and are easily totable for a healthy workday snack, too.

1   Preheat the oven to 180°C.

2   In a bowl, mix all of the ingredients together with 250 ml (1 cup) of water and set aside for 15 minutes for the water to soak in.

3   Take a third of the mixture and roll it out to 2 mm thick between two sheets of baking paper on a baking tray. Repeat to roll out the remaining mixture on separate trays.

4   Remove the top sheet of baking paper and bake for 20–25 minutes until golden brown around the edges.

5   Cool completely before using your hands to break it into bite-size chunks.

105 g (1 cup) rolled oats
50 g (½ cup) psyllium husks
75 g (½ cup) linseeds (flaxseeds)
75 g (½ cup) sunflower seeds
40 g (¼ cup) chia seeds
40 g (¼ cup) black sesame seeds
1 teaspoon sea salt flakes
3 tablespoons coconut oil

*Pair with hummus (see page 86) + vegie sticks, olives and some milk-poached chicken (see page 50) for an epic meze plate.*

**Make**
Want to get creative? Divide the dough into three bowls and add different dried herbs and spices before rolling.

**Save**
Lasts 1 week in an airtight container at room temperature.

**Tip**
If you don't have a rolling pin, use the roll of baking paper with a couple of rubber bands around it to stop it unravelling.

STEP 2 **BATCH AND STASH**

# Zucchini fritters

**Portions** 4 | **Hands-on prep time** 10 minutes

This is a clever way to get everyone to eat more vegies. It's a super-versatile recipe, too: serve these as a side dish or stack them high for a filling weekend breakfast.

2 zucchini, grated or spiralised
2 large eggs, lightly beaten
40 g (⅓ cup) coconut flour
2 spring onions (scallions), sliced
¼ cup chopped fresh herbs
½ teaspoon sea salt

¼ teaspoon freshly ground black pepper
2 tablespoons coconut oil, for frying

1   Put the zucchini in a bowl with the eggs, coconut flour, spring onion, herbs, salt and pepper. Mix well until combined. If the mixture is too wet to shape, add a little more flour. If the mixture is too dry, add a little more egg.

2   Heat the coconut oil in a large frying pan over medium–high heat. When the oil is hot, add 2 tablespoons of mixture to the pan and repeat with remaining mixture. Fill the base of the pan but don't let the individual fritters stick together.

3   Fry for about 3 minutes on each side until golden brown. Remove fritters from the pan and drain on paper towel.

*I love adding extra flavour with chopped coriander*

**Save**

Store fritters on a layer of paper towel in an airtight container in the fridge for up to 4 days, or freeze for up to 1 month. The paper towel will help keep them crispy.

**Tip**

If you prefer, replace the coconut flour with almond meal or buckwheat flour.

STEP 2 **BATCH AND STASH**

# Whole roasted pumpkin

**Portions** 10   |   **Hands-on prep time** 10 minutes

Pumpkin is one of my favourite ingredients. It's sweet, smoky, packed with nutrients and super versatile in both savoury and sweet dishes. Leaving the skin on intensifies the flavour – plus there's minimum effort.

1  Preheat the oven to 200°C.

2  Drizzle the olive oil over the pumpkin, then rub all over to coat.

3  Wrap the pumpkin in baking paper and then foil. Set it directly on the middle shelf of the oven and bake for 2–2½ hours until tender.

4  Unwrap and roast for another 30 minutes until the skin is dark.

5  Remove the pumpkin from the oven and set it aside to cool completely.

6  Cut the pumpkin into wedges or scoop out the soft flesh (discarding the seeds) and mash it.

2 kg whole Japanese pumpkin
3 tablespoons olive oil

### Easy eating options

* Stir mashed pumpkin into oats with cinnamon and a drizzle of maple syrup for a delicious brekkie.
* Mash with miso paste and serve with salmon and steamed greens for a quick dinner.
* Use in muffin recipes to replace some of the flour and keep them deliciously moist.
* Cut a small wedge and serve with plain yoghurt, chopped pecans, chopped dates and sea salt for an afternoon snack.
* Add heated coconut milk or water, soy sauce or tamari and peanut butter then blend for a deliciously simple Asian-style pumpkin soup.

**Save**

Store cooked pumpkin flesh in an airtight container in the fridge for up to 1 week. Freeze portions in icetrays for up to 6 months and pop out frozen cubes when needed.

*Peeling, scooping and cubing your pumpkin before cooking? I'm over it!*

STEP 2 BATCH AND STASH

# The perfect roast veg

**Portions** 6–8  |  **Hands-on prep time** 15 minutes

Meal prep is all about speed. Roasted veg can take ages in the oven, but it's possible to speed up the process. If you're in a serious hurry, opt for vegies grown ABOVE ground for faster roasting times.

1. Preheat the oven to 200°C. Use silicone mats or foil to line 3 baking trays.

2. Sort vegetables into similar types on each tray, so that they finish roasting at the same time – that way you can remove each tray when it's ready. Pair root vegetables such as sweet potato, parsnip, turnips and carrots together. Brussels sprouts, broccoli and cauliflower go together; and softer vegies such as zucchini, onion, eggplant, leek and capsicum go on the final tray.

3. Cut all your vegies so they're about the same size. The smaller the pieces, the faster they roast.

4. Spread the vegies on the trays in one layer. Don't overlap or stack them; they should all have contact with the baking tray.

5. Drizzle each tray with one-third of the olive oil (3 tablespoons). The oil helps to transfer heat and adds good fat that allows our bodies make the most of the fat-soluble vitamins in the vegies.

6. Sprinkle evenly with the sea salt and roast, removing trays as the vegies are cooked. Cool completely before storing in the fridge.

Seasonal vegies, scrubbed but not peeled
185 ml (¾ cup) olive oil
1½ tablespoons sea salt

*Toss roasted vegies into the food processor with the Hummus recipe (see page 86)*

 **Make**
To reheat vegies, put them in a saucepan with a squeeze of lemon juice to stop them from sticking to the base. Stir regularly for 5 minutes until warmed through. Alternatively, enjoy them cold with salad (my favourite), or with poachies on top.

 **Save**
Store in containers in the fridge for 3–4 days. You can separate the different vegies or just toss them all into one large container.

 **Tip**
Want to halve the roasting time? Steam the vegies until tender before roasting.

STEP 2 **BATCH AND STASH**

# Sticky and sugarless caramelised onions

**Portions** 10–12  |  **Hands-on prep time** 15 minutes

These make a great base for so many dishes. They can be reheated or enjoyed cold. Throw them on top of turkey rissoles or fish cakes, add them to curries, toast, soup and more.

8 white or red onions, peeled
2 tablespoons olive oil

1 teaspoon sea salt flakes

1. Start by halving each onion through the root. Using a sharp knife, cut a V-shape around the root to remove it. Place the onion flat-side down on a chopping board and slice thinly from one side to the other, or use a mandolin.

2. Heat the olive oil in a wide-based pan (so the onion has room to caramelise, not steam). Add half the onion and cook, stirring, for 1–2 minutes until soft and turning translucent. Add the remaining onion and season with sea salt.

3. Reduce the heat to medium–low and stir occasionally for 15–20 minutes until the onion is very soft. If it starts to stick to the pan, add a splash of hot water and stir.

4. Cool in the pan and then transfer to an airtight container.

**Save**

Store in an airtight container in the fridge for up to 7 days.

**Tip**

Use bent fingers to hold the bulk of the onion in place. Your knuckles will act as a knife guard.

STEP 2 **BATCH AND STASH**

# Sweet and savoury gluten-free pie crusts

**Makes** 20 cm pie crust  |  **Hands-on prep time** 20 minutes

This recipe is also dairy free and vegan, so you can feed it to everyone! Double the mix and freeze half the dough, or cook the spare crust and freeze it to fill later.

1. Preheat the oven to 200°C. Grease a 20 cm round pie dish with olive oil or coconut oil spray and set aside.

2. In a large bowl, combine all the basic crust ingredients and mix, kneading with your hands when a dough ball forms. If necessary, add a little almond milk (if your dough is a bit dry) or flour (if it's sticky) — use your judgement here.

3. Roll the dough on a flat surface until it's large enough to cover the pie dish. I like to roll mine between two sheets of baking paper, but you can dust your rolling pin and work surface with flour for a similar nonstick situation.

4. Transfer the crust to the pie dish and gently press to fit.

5. Cut away any excess dough with scissors or a knife and bake the crust for 15 minutes.

6. Fill as desired: for a sweet option try Canadian pumpkin pie (see page 110) or for savoury, the Apple + goat's cheese + sage quiche (see page 108).

### Basic crust

165 g (1¼ cups) buckwheat flour, plus extra for dusting and rolling
125 g (1¼ cups) almond meal
125 ml (½ cup) unsweetened almond milk
60 ml (¼ cup) avocado oil or coconut oil (melted)
½ teaspoon sea salt flakes
⅛ teaspoon baking powder

### Sweet crust

+ 1 tablespoon maple syrup

### Savoury crust

+ 1 tablespoon dried herbs or nutritional yeast

*for extra yum*

**Save**
Freeze baked crusts covered in plastic wrap for up to 1 month, or freeze dough for up to 3 months.

STEP 2 **BATCH AND STASH**

# Apple + goat's cheese + sage quiche

**Serves 8**  |  **Hands-on prep time** 20 minutes

A good quiche is the mainstay of many café menus. I grew up on the stuff. Instead of boring bacon and cheddar, try it with this delicious flavour combo.

1. Preheat the oven to 180°C.

2. Mix the eggs, milk and rosemary in a bowl.

3. Pour the egg mixture into the precooked pie crust and drop teaspoons of the cheese over the top.

4. Finally, lay the apple slices on top, and bake for 35–45 minutes until set.

5. Cool for 5 minutes before removing from the dish and slicing. Garnish with extra rosemary to serve.

12 eggs
60 ml (¼ cup) milk of your choice
1 tablespoon fresh rosemary leaves, plus extra sprigs to serve
1 cooked Savoury gluten-free pie crust (see page 106)
80 g goat's cheese, or feta cheese
1 small green apple, thinly sliced

**Save**
Store in the fridge for 3–4 days. Egg dishes can't be frozen, so make this dish with mates in mind.

**Tip**
If you have time, sauté some leeks and add them to the egg mixture.

STEP 2 **BATCH AND STASH**

# Canadian pumpkin pie

Serves 8 | Hands-on prep time 15 minutes

I went to Canada recently, and was told SO much about their pumpkin pie. I headed into a famous restaurant where they were serving said pie, with spray-on cream. Not one to miss out, I ordered a piece to share with a travel buddy. While it was delicious, it was all kinds of unhealthy, with condensed milk and white sugar. Not the kind of thing I want to be noshing on, on the regular. This is a simple, healthier take on that mouthwatering pie.

1 Preheat the oven to 180°C.

2 Mix together the pumpkin, eggs, maple syrup, coconut milk, vanilla, salt and spices. Pour into the precooked pie crust.

3 Bake for 50 minutes. Meanwhile, mix together the ingredients for the Vanilla maple yoghurt.

4 Cool the pie before removing from the tin. Serve with a dollop of Vanilla maple yoghurt, scattered with star anise, cinnamon, salt and nutmeg.

2 cups cooked mashed pumpkin (see page 100)
3 large eggs
125 ml (½ cup) maple syrup, honey or granulated stevia
200 ml tinned full-fat coconut milk
½ teaspoon vanilla extract
¼ teaspoon sea salt
½ teaspoon ground nutmeg
1 teaspoon ground allspice
2 teaspoons ground cinnamon
1 cooked Sweet gluten-free pie crust (see page 106)
Star anise, cinnamon sticks, salt and freshly grated nutmeg, to serve

Vanilla maple yoghurt

260 g (1 cup) coconut yoghurt or plain Greek yoghurt
1 teaspoon vanilla bean paste or extract
1 tablespoon maple syrup

**Save**

Store the pie in the fridge for up to 4 days or freeze for up to 1 month. Mix up the yoghurt ingredients just before eating.

STEP 2 **BATCH AND STASH**

# Cauliflower pizza bases

*Save half and enjoy it cold for a quick brekkie*

Serves 2 | Hands-on prep time 10 minutes | One pizza = 2 portions

These recipes are for one pizza base, but I highly recommend doubling or tripling the quantities listed, and sticking the extra bases in the freezer for a super-fast dinner.

1. Preheat the oven to 180°C. Line a baking tray with a silicone mat or baking paper.

2. If you are making the vegan version, make a 'flax egg' by soaking the linseed meal in 2½ tablespoons of water for 5 minutes.

3. Meanwhile, turn the cauliflower into 'rice' by grating it (a kitchen grater is fine and easy to clean, but a food processor does an ace job too). You should have about 3 cups of rice.

4. Soften the cauli in a frying pan over medium heat for 8–10 minutes, stirring with a splash of water so it doesn't stick. (This is optional, but makes your base extra crispy by allowing you to squeeze more water out.)

5. Throw it into a clean tea towel or muslin cloth and squeeze the cauliflower to drain it of as much water as humanly possible. Annoying, but you can count it towards your workout.

6. Put the cauli into a bowl with the remaining ingredients (including the 'flax egg' if you are making the vegan version) and mix until fully combined.

7. Press the mix into a rectangle on the lined baking tray. Cook for 30–40 minutes until golden brown.

8. Top with your favourite pizza toppings and bake for another 10 minutes. Or allow the untopped base to cool, then freeze it.

### Vegan
1 tablespoon linseed (flaxseed) meal (to make a 'flax egg')
1 large cauliflower
30 g (¼ cup) besan (chickpea flour)
1 teaspoon dried oregano
½ teaspoon sea salt

### Non-vegan
1 large cauliflower
2 tablespoons grated parmesan cheese
1 teaspoon dried oregano
½ teaspoon sea salt
Option: omit the cheese and add an egg

**Save**
If you plan on freezing a few bases at a time, put baking paper between them to prevent them from sticking together. Freeze for up to 2 months. When you're hungry, just whip out a frozen base, bake for 10 minutes, then top with your faves and bake again for another 10 minutes.

**Tip**
It's much easier to make (and store) rectangular pizza bases.

STEP 2 **BATCH AND STASH**

# Leftover vegetable bake

Portions 6  |  Hands-on prep time 10 minutes

When you get to the end of the week and your salad bar is looking a bit sad and sorry, dice up what's left and throw into a baking dish along with any limp-looking herbs. The majority of food waste is unnecessary and it costs us all a lot of hard-hard-earned cash.

1  Preheat the oven to 180°C.

2  Slice or chop the veg and toss them together in a baking dish.

3  Mix together the eggs, herbs, milk and any flavour bombs you like (see pages 20–23) and pour it over the vegetables.

4  Top with parmesan (if using) and bake for 30–40 minutes until set in the middle.

5  Cool for 10 minutes before devouring.

2 cups leftover cooked vegies
12 eggs
½ cup leftover fresh herbs, chopped
125 ml (½ cup) milk of your choice
25 g (¼ cup) finely grated parmesan cheese (optional)

**Save**
Keep in the fridge for 2–3 days.

**Tip**
Make this into portable snacks by using a silicone muffin tin instead and reducing the baking time.

STEP 2 **BATCH AND STASH**

# Marinated chickpeas

Portions 2 | Hands-on prep time 5 minutes

This high-protein bowl of goodness is so easy to prepare and it's delicious as a snack or a side dish.

1. Put the chickpeas into a bowl, along with the onion.
2. Add the cumin, coriander, olive oil, salt and vinegar. Mix well.
3. Cover and refrigerate.

400 g tin chickpeas, rinsed and drained
1 small red onion, thinly sliced
1 teaspoon cumin seeds
1 teaspoon coriander seeds
1 tablespoon olive oil
½ teaspoon sea salt
2 tablespoons red wine vinegar
Fresh thyme leaves, to serve

**Make**

Save the liquid from the can (it's called aquafaba). It can be whisked into peaks like egg white. Try using it in the Nut clusters recipe (see page 138) for a vegan egg white replacement.

**Save**

Keep for up to 5 days in the fridge, or freeze for up to 1 month.

**Tip**

Make the recipe with tinned lentils instead of chickpeas. Prepare both at the same time to keep your options open at each meal.

STEP 2 BATCH AND STASH

# Anchovy + broccoli + pear soup

Portions 4  |  Hands-on prep time 25 minutes

This is an awesome way to get acquainted with broccoli: a nice balance of salty anchovies and sweet pear helps to elevate broccoli to another level in this soup!

1. Heat a large saucepan or stockpot over medium heat and add the olive oil, onion and garlic. Sauté for 5 minutes until softened, but not coloured. If using Caramelised onions, you're just warming these through.

2. Chop broccoli into small florets and thinly slice the stems. Add to the pan along with the pear.

3. Pour in the stock or water and bring to a fast simmer, then drop the heat down and gently bubble for 15 minutes or until the broccoli and pear are soft.

4. Add the anchovies and white pepper, and blitz with a stick blender until smooth.

5. Remove from the heat and pour in the coconut milk, then stir until well combined.

6. Keep warm and drizzle with coconut milk. Serve sprinkled with herbs, walnuts and chia seeds, plus a slice of Paleo bread (see page 90).

2 tablespoons olive oil
2 white onions, chopped (or ½ cup Caramelised onions – see page 104)
2 garlic cloves, finely sliced
2 medium broccoli, including stems (about 500 g)
2 pears, cored and coarsely chopped
1 litre (4 cups) stock or water
12 anchovies
½ teaspoon ground white pepper
250 ml (1 cup) tinned coconut milk, plus extra to drizzle
Fresh herbs, chopped walnuts and chia seeds, to serve

Save
Keep in the fridge for 4–5 days. Freeze for up to 2 months.

STEP 2 **BATCH AND STASH**

# DIY vinaigrettes

**Hands-on prep time** 5 minutes

### Mix

Make a large batch of vinaigrette (say, 1 cup of vinegar and 3 cups of oil) in a glass jar; secure the lid and shake. Want an individual portion? Follow the same formula, using tablespoons instead of cups, and whisk with a fork in a small bowl.

### Taste

Taste and adjust the flavour to your personal tastes. Need more salt? Lemon? Best to do this by dipping in a salad leaf or vegie stick rather than going in neat.

### Store

If you have only used oil, vinegar, salt and pepper, you can store this in the cupboard in a glass jar for 2–3 weeks. If you've used fresh ingredients (from the fridge) such as lemon or herbs, store in the fridge for up to 5 days.

# ALL the dressings

**Makes** about 250 ml (1 cup)  |  **Hands-on prep time** 5–10 minutes

The right dressing can really make or break a dish. I use dressing on nearly everything I eat: roast vegies, eggs, chicken, steamed greens, you name it.

1. Blend or stir all the ingredients together and store in an airtight container in the fridge for up to 1 week. I use clean recycled glass jars so I can shake them easily.

### Pea + almond pesto

1 cup fresh or defrosted frozen peas + 1 cup almonds + 2 garlic cloves + ½ bunch fresh mint, leaves picked + 1 bunch fresh basil, leaves picked + 125 ml (½ cup) extra virgin olive oil + salt + pepper to taste

### The simple one

260 g (1 cup) plain yoghurt + 3 tablespoons dijon mustard + 2 teaspoons sriracha

### Lemon + tahini

### Lemon + tahini

135 g (½ cup) tahini
+ 125 ml (½ cup) warm water
+ 3 tablespoons lemon juice
+ 1 teaspoon sea salt
+ 2 garlic cloves, crushed

### Miso + almond

140 g (½ cup) almond butter + 80 ml (⅓ cup) warm water + 2 tablespoons apple cider vinegar + 1 tablespoon miso paste + 1 tablespoon sesame oil + 1 tablespoon raw honey or maple syrup (optional) + 2 garlic cloves, crushed

### Coconut tzatziki

260 g (1 cup) coconut yoghurt + ¼ cup finely chopped cucumber + 3 tablespoons lemon juice + 1 tablespoon chopped dill + ½ teaspoon sea salt

### The green one

4 tablespoons lime juice + 4 tablespoons tahini + 3 tablespoons extra virgin olive oil + 2 tablespoons mustard + 1 bunch fresh coriander, leaves picked + 1 teaspoon ground ginger + 1 teaspoon ground coriander + 1 tablespoon honey or 10 drops liquid stevia + salt + pepper

# Quick pickles

Portions 6–8 per jar  |  **Hands-on prep time** 10 minutes per jar

I love quick pickles (aka refrigerator pickles). They don't produce the deep flavour (or bacterial goodness) of their fermented counterparts, BUT they're ready in a few hours and save you precious time 'canning' them. Store them in the refrigerator, and throw them onto anything you like: salads, savoury oats, fish dishes, goddess bowls – you get the picture.

Did you know? White vinegar shares similar health properties to the revered apple cider version. Both are high in acetic acid, which is said to kill harmful bacteria, stabilise blood sugar, and slow the digestion to keep you fuller for longer.

1. Combine the vinegar, mustard seeds and cumin seeds in a large saucepan. Bring to the boil over medium–high heat.

2. Pack the chopped vegies into clean glass jars, leaving a little space at the top for vinegar to completely immerse them.

3. Pour the hot liquid over the vegies until the jar is full. Cool the jars to room temperature, then secure the lids and refrigerate.

**Save**
Pickled vegies can be eaten after a few short hours, but will last up to 1 month in the fridge.

*Rainbow chard*

*Fennel + fronds + stems*

### Pickle liquid

For a 1 litre jar
(quantities are approximate)
500 ml (2 cups) white vinegar
½ teaspoon mustard seeds
½ teaspoon cumin seeds
½ teaspoon sea salt

### My favourite vegie combos

4 cups sliced, chopped or julienned vegetables
* celery + cucumber + cauliflower
* carrot + carrot tops + radish
* fennel + fronds + stems
* red onion
* whatever you have on hand

*Carrot + carrot tops + radish*

*Celery + cauliflower*

*Red onion*

*Celery*

*Rainbow chard*

STEP 2 **BATCH AND STASH**

# DIY trail mix

**Portions** 5 (30 g serves)  |  **Hands-on prep time** 10 minutes

**NUTS + SEEDS** (1 cup total, any combination)

Cashews  Macadamias  Pine nuts  Almonds  Pepitas  Brazil nuts  Sunflower seeds  Pistachios  Peanuts

**+**

**YUMMY BITS** (½ cup total, any combination)

Cacao nibs  Dried figs  Puffed rice  Shredded coconut  Raisins  Buckwheat  Puffed millet  Dried blueberries, mulberries, or cherries

**+**

**FLAVOUR BOMBS** (2 teaspoons)

Sweet

Cacao  Cinnamon  Citrus zest  Ginger  Maca powder  Vanilla powder

Savoury

Sea salt  Chilli  Paprika  Herbs  Pepper  Garlic powder

**Save**

Store in an airtight container at room temperature for 6 months. Freeze for up to 2 years.

**Tip**

Put all of the ingredients into a jar or large resealable plastic bag and SHAKE.

*Cashews + Shredded coconut + Lime zest + Chilli flakes*

*Almonds + Cacao nibs + Coconut flakes + Cacao powder*

*Pine nuts + Macadamias + Chopped dried figs + Finely chopped rosemary + Sea salt flakes*

# Sweet + savoury freezer truffles

Portions 10 (2 dates) | Hands-on prep time 10 minutes

Ever feel like you just need a little sumthin' sumthin' to round off a meal, but you're probably not actually hungry? Rather than reach for the nearest chocolate bar, these little mouthfuls are awesome to have in your freezer. Freezing the dates firms them up and makes them deliciously chewy, just like a proper caramel. STUFF THEM WITH YUMMY THINGS in less than a minute and devour. Perfection.

1. Grab a few cups of medjool dates (the big, juicy ones) and pit them all.

2. Chuck them in an airtight container and freeze (for up to 2 months).

3. When you want a quick snack or after-dinner treat, grab a few and stuff them with some of your favourite fillings. Ideas below.

### Savoury

- 1 walnut + 1 teaspoon blue cheese
- 1 olive + 1 teaspoon hummus (see page 86)
- Basil leaf + small cube of cheddar cheese

### Sweet

- 1 teaspoon almond butter + sea salt
- 1 pecan + 1 square of dark chocolate
- 1 teaspoon coconut butter + ground cinnamon

STEP 2 BATCH AND STASH

# Salted chocolate banana bread

**Portions** 12  |  **Hands-on prep time** 20 minutes

I'd never tried banana bread until I moved to Australia. It's a blessing in disguise: delicious but often packed with refined flour and sugar. This version, however, is not! I have this toasted for a weekend brekkie and keep slices in the freezer ready to go.

1. Preheat the oven to 180°C. Line a loaf tin with baking paper or use a silicone loaf tin.

2. In a large bowl, mix the nut meal, cacao powder, baking powder, bicarbonate of soda, salt, and cinnamon. Set aside.

3. In a separate bowl, beat together the eggs, coconut sugar, coconut oil, vanilla and milk. Fold in the mashed banana.

4. Pour the wet ingredients into the bowl with the dry ingredients, mixing well.

5. Pour the batter into the loaf tin, arrange the two banana halves on top, and sprinkle with the salt.

6. Bake for 1 hour or until a knife inserted in the centre comes out clean.

7. Cool in the tin before turning out and slicing.

125 g (1¼ cups) almond or hazelnut meal
65 g (½ cup) cacao powder, sifted
1 teaspoon baking powder
1 teaspoon bicarbonate of soda
2 teaspoons sea salt
2 teaspoons ground cinnamon
2 large eggs
50 g (⅓ cup) coconut sugar
80 ml (⅓ cup) melted coconut oil
2 teaspoons vanilla extract
1½ tablespoons milk of your choice
5 bananas, mashed

### Topping
1 large banana, halved lengthways
1 teaspoon sea salt flakes

**Save**

Store in an airtight container in the fridge for 3–4 days. Slice and freeze between pieces of baking paper for up to 6 weeks.

STEP 2 **BATCH AND STASH**

# Salted caramel

**Makes** 1 jar (about 12 portions)  |  **Hands-on prep time** 5 minutes

Throw this on your overnight oats, on pancakes and waffles, spread it on a banana as a snack, or add a tablespoon to smoothies.

1. Put all of the ingredients except the salt in a food processor and blitz until smooth, or stick it in a bowl and get whisking to make it lump-free.

2. Stir the salt flakes through and transfer to a glass jar.

125 ml (½ cup) **maple syrup**
125 ml (½ cup) **tinned coconut milk**
125 ml (½ cup) **melted coconut oil**
90 g (⅓ cup) **natural almond butter**
1½ teaspoons **sea salt flakes**

**Save**

Store at room temperature for up to 1 week. Freeze leftovers in an icetray and add to smoothies.

STEP 2 **BATCH AND STASH**

# Cardamom + chocolate + cherry tray-baked oats

**Portions** 10  |  **Hands-on prep time** 15 minutes

Admittedly this recipe has a few more ingredients than I'd usually bother with, but I promise it's oh-so-worth it. It doubles as breakfast and dessert.

1 Preheat the oven to 180°C.

2 In a mixing bowl, combine the oats, nuts, cinnamon, cacao, baking powder, salt and cardamom.

3 Make a well in the centre and add the milk, egg, sweetener, butter or oil and vanilla. Mix these together before incorporating the oat mixture.

4 Add the cherries and chocolate chips (if using) and give it all a good stir.

5 Pour the mix into a deep baking tray and spread it out with the back of a spoon. Mine is usually about 2.5 cm thick, but if yours is thinner you can shave off a bit of the bake time.

6 Bake for 45 minutes, then remove and cool for 5 minutes before spooning some into a bowl and devouring.

210 g (2 cups) rolled oats
85 g (⅔ cup) coarsely chopped pecans or almonds
2 teaspoons ground cinnamon
25 g (¼ cup) cacao powder
1 teaspoon baking powder
½ teaspoon sea salt
1 teaspoon ground cardamom
500 ml (2 cups) milk of your choice
3 large eggs or 'flax eggs' (see page 112)
80 ml (⅓ cup) maple syrup, honey or granulated stevia
3 tablespoons melted butter or coconut oil
2 teaspoons vanilla extract
2½ cups cherries (fresh or frozen)
85 g (½ cup) dark chocolate chips or cacao nibs (optional)

*No cherries? Try blackberries, blueberries or raspberries*

**Make**
Optional toppings for serving: plain yoghurt + a drizzle of maple syrup or honey + extra choc chips or cacao nibs.

**Save**
Store in an airtight container in the fridge for up to 1 week. Freeze as individual portions for up to 2 months.

STEP 2 **BATCH AND STASH**

# Raspberry + peanut butter mud slice

**Portions** 12  |  **Hands-on prep time** 15 minutes

Kinda like a deliciously moist brownie, this slice pretends to be a decadent treat. Don't let it fool you: it's sugar-free and packed with fibre for healthy digestion.

1. Preheat the oven to 180°C. Line a 22 x 28 cm brownie pan with baking paper.

2. Put the cannellini beans and peanut butter in a food processor and blend until smooth, then add the almond meal, baking powder, eggs, vanilla, stevia and salt.

3. Fold the raspberries through the batter and pour it into the brownie pan. Scatter a handful of peanuts on top, if using.

4. Bake for 45–50 minutes until the centre is just set.

5. Cool completely before cutting into squares.

400 g tin cannellini (or other white) beans, drained and rinsed
140 g (½ cup) peanut butter
100 g (1 cup) almond meal
1 teaspoon baking powder
3 large eggs or 'flax eggs' (see page 112)
2 teaspoons vanilla extract
120 g (⅔ cup) granulated stevia
½ teaspoon sea salt
150 g raspberries (frozen or fresh)
Peanuts, to scatter (optional)

**Save**

Store in an airtight container in the fridge for up to 5 days. Freeze for up to 2 months.

STEP 2 **BATCH AND STASH**

# Nut clusters

Makes 30 | Hands-on prep time 10 minutes

Packed with fibre, vitamins and antioxidants, nuts are in my diet every day. Portion control is important with these clusters: try not to eat half the batch in one sitting!

1. Preheat the oven to 180°C. Line 2 large baking trays with baking paper.

2. In a bowl, whisk the egg whites until frothy, then fold in the nuts, fruit, cinnamon and salt, until well coated.

3. Spoon large dollops of mixture onto the baking trays and bake for 10 minutes or until golden. Cool on the trays.

3 egg whites
600 g unsalted mixed nuts
150 g dried fruit, such as figs and raisins, chopped
1–2 teaspoons ground cinnamon
1 teaspoon sea salt (optional)

*I love cashews, almonds, pistachios and pine nuts*

**Save**
Store in the fridge for up to 1 week. Keep them in the freezer for up to 1 month, for the best portion control!

**Tip**
Make chocolatey versions by adding 2 teaspoons of cacao powder instead of the cinnamon.

STEP 2 **BATCH AND STASH**

# Blender cookie dough

Portions 10 | Hands-on prep time 10 minutes

This is my favourite Friday-night treat. Arguably healthier than a tub of a certain cookie dough ice cream that I used to indulge in way too often. Zero guilt allowed.

1. Put the oats, cashews and almond meal into a food processor, and blend to the consistency of flour.

2. Add melted coconut oil and honey or maple syrup and process again.

3. Remove from the food processor and stir in the chocolate chips or cacao nibs.

4. Store in an airtight container in the fridge for up to 2 weeks, so you'll be ready when sweet cravings hit.

75 g (¾ cup) rolled oats
120 g (¾ cup) cashews (or more oats)
150 g (1½ cups) almond meal
3 tablespoons coconut oil
4 tablespoons honey or maple syrup
85 g (½ cup) chocolate chips or cacao nibs

**Save**

These are freezer-friendly, so if you struggle with portion control like me, roll into balls or press into cubes and freeze for up to 3 months.

STEP 2 **BATCH AND STASH**

# Fruit crumble duo

Portions 6 | Hands-on prep time 20 minutes

Oh crumble! Our love affair has been long and wonderful. When I can't decide which filling I want, I make two in one pan. That's genius right there.

1 Preheat the oven to 180°C.

**For the crumble**

2 In a large bowl, mix the oats, almond meal, cinnamon and salt.

3 Next, add the coconut oil or butter and rub the mix together between your fingers until a crumbly biscuit texture forms.

4 Add the sweetener (if using) and stir with a wooden spoon.

**For the fruit**

5 Set two small saucepans over medium heat. Put the blackberries in one and the apple in the other, along with 125 ml (½ cup) of water (hot from the kettle to speed things up) in each saucepan.

6 Stir in half the stevia and half the lemon juice to each pan.

7 Gently simmer, uncovered, for 8–10 minutes until the fruit is soft and the liquid has reduced by half.

8 Spoon the blackberries into one side of a baking dish, and spoon the apple into the other side. Don't worry if the juices mix together; it will all taste delicious.

9 Add the crumble topping and bake for 30 minutes or until the topping is golden brown.

**Crumble**
160 g (1½ cups) rolled oats
100 g (1 cup) almond meal
2 teaspoons ground cinnamon
1 teaspoon sea salt
3 tablespoons coconut oil (solid) or butter
3 tablespoons rice malt syrup or sweetener of your choice (optional)

**Filling**
3 cups blackberries (fresh or frozen)
3 cups chopped apple
1 lemon
½ cup granulated stevia or other sweetener

*Add the lemon zest too, for extra zing*

**Save**
Store in the fridge for 5 days; freeze for up to 2 months.

**Tip**
If you live in a warm country like Australia, pop coconut oil in the fridge for a couple of hours to keep it solid.

# Two-ingredient sweet treats

*Coconut fudge bites*
*Sweet crackers*

| | | | | |
|---|---|---|---|---|
| **Peanut butter ice cream** | 1 tablespoon peanut butter | **+** | 1 cup frozen banana | **+** Mix + blend |

| | | | | |
|---|---|---|---|---|
| **Coconut fudge bites** | 2½ tablespoons coconut butter | **+** | 1 cup pitted dates | **+** Blend + roll |

| | | | | |
|---|---|---|---|---|
| **Chocolate proghurt** | 130 g (½ cup) plain yoghurt | **+** | 30 g (1 scoop) chocolate protein powder | **+** Mix |

| | | | | |
|---|---|---|---|---|
| **Nana cookies** | 1 mashed banana | **+** | 55 g (½ cup) rolled oats | **+** Mix + bake at 180°C until golden |

| | | | | |
|---|---|---|---|---|
| **Sweet crackers** | 1 mashed banana | **+** | ½ cup linseeds (flaxseeds) | **+** Mix + bake at 180°C until golden |

| | | | | |
|---|---|---|---|---|
| **Pineapple ice** | Frozen pineapple chunks | **+** | Fresh mint leaves | **+** Blend |

STEP 2 BATCH AND STASH

# DIY bliss balls

Makes 15 | Hands-on prep time 10 minutes

### BASE (1 cup total, any combination)

| Whole nuts | Flour | Grains | Other dry stuff |
|---|---|---|---|
| Cashews | Almond meal | Rolled oats | Sunflower seeds |
| Almonds | Hazelnut meal | Quinoa flakes | Pepitas (pumpkin seeds) |
| Walnuts | Oat flour | Spelt flakes | Desiccated coconut |
| Pistachios | | | |

**+**

### BINDER (¾ cup total, any combination)

Dates | Raisins | Dried apricots | Prunes | Dried figs | Cranberries

**+**

### NUT OR SEED BUTTER (¼ cup)

Almond butter | Peanut butter | Tahini | Sunflower seed butter | Walnut butter | Cashew butter

**+**

### FLAVOUR BOMBS (½ teaspoon)

Cinnamon | Ground coffee | Vanilla | Sea salt | Citrus zest | Orange oil | Ground ginger | Peppermint oil

*Pulse it together. Roll into balls*

### COATINGS

Chopped nuts | Desiccated coconut | Cacao nibs | Chia seeds | Sesame seeds | Cacao powder

STEP 2 **BATCH AND STASH**

# Four-ingredient chocolate chip cookies

**Makes** 15 | **Hands-on prep time** 15 minutes

You can't have a meal-prep plan without cookies: where's the balance in that? Keep it simple and nutritious with these four ingredients.

1 Preheat the oven to 180°C. Line a baking tray with baking paper.

2 Put the tahini and maple syrup into a saucepan over low heat.

3 Mix until well combined, remove from the heat and stir in the almond meal and cacao nibs or chocolate chips.

4 Scoop out a heaped tablespoon of dough and roll it into a ball between your hands, then place on the prepared baking tray and press down with your hands to flatten. Sprinkle with salt, if using.

5 Bake for 10–12 minutes and cool before transferring to an airtight container.

270 g (1 cup) tahini
80 ml (⅓ cup) maple syrup
200 g (2 cups) almond meal
3 tablespoons cacao nibs or dark chocolate chips
½ teaspoon sea salt (optional)

**Save**
Store in the fridge for up to 7 days, or freeze for up to 1 month.

*Step 3*

# PUT IT TOGETHER

STEP 3 PUT IT TOGETHER

# Poached egg combos

I love eggs for breakfast, lunch and dinner! Keep them interesting with these combos. Combo 1 adds spring onion and chilli to yoghurt for a surprisingly zingy flavour fest.

## COMBO 1

Poached egg — Page 45 + Paleo bread — Page 90 + Yoghurt + Parsley

PLUS spring onion, chilli flakes, sesame seeds, paprika

## COMBO 2

Poached egg — Page 45 + Salmon gravlax — Page 40 + Avocado + Lemon juice

## COMBO 3

Poached egg — Page 45 + Spicy beef mince — Page 70 + Salad greens + Brown rice — Page 89

STEP 3 PUT IT TOGETHER

# Salmon gravlax combos

Gravlax is the ultimate easy-to-make luxury food. Use sushi-grade salmon for the best results. Pair it with sharp flavours and contrasting textures for a memorable meal or snack.

## COMBO 1

Salmon gravlax — Page 40 **+** Zucchini fritters — Page 98 **+** Coconut tzatziki dressing — Page 123 **+** Pepper

**PLUS** lemon zest, dill

## COMBO 2

Salmon gravlax — Page 40 **+** Oaty seed crackers — Page 96 **+** Goat's cheese **+** Pepper

## COMBO 3

Salmon gravlax — Page 40 **+** Pickled onion **+** Chopped pistachios **+** Sour cream **+** Flax waffles — Page 92

STEP 3 PUT IT TOGETHER

# Falafel combos

This Middle Eastern fave is a dish even non-vegos love. Perfect served simply with hummus or a tangy dressing, falafel is even better with these combos.

## COMBO 1

| Nut butter falafel | Hummus | Corn tortilla | Pea + almond pesto |
| Page 54 | Page 86 | | Page 122 |

PLUS red onion, cucumber, herbs

## COMBO 2

Nut butter falafel   Marinated chickpeas   Salad greens   Coconut tzatziki   Dried apricots,
Page 54              Page 116                             dressing Page 123  chopped

## COMBO 3

Nut butter falafel   Perfect roast veg   Black bean hummus   Olive oil
Page 54              Page 102            Page 86

STEP 3 PUT IT TOGETHER

# Smoky turkey rissole combos

Turkey meat helps support healthy levels of serotonin in the body, which makes it good mood food. Try making turkey mince into burgers, meatballs or rissoles and eating them in a salad, with vegies or — my favourite — on Flax waffles.

## COMBO 1

Smoky turkey rissoles Page 66 + Flax waffles Page 92 + Pea + almond pesto Page 122 + Salad greens

**PLUS** tomatoes, dried chilli flakes, black pepper, herbs

## COMBO 2

Smoky turkey rissoles Page 66 + Spiralised vegies + The green one dressing Page 123 + Tomatoes

## COMBO 3

Smoky turkey rissoles Page 66 + Perfect roast veg Page 102 + Quinoa Page 89 + Avocado + Coriander

STEP 3 PUT IT TOGETHER

# Healthy fish cake combos

These fish cakes are a hero in your fridge. Pair with a crisp salad and a squeeze of lemon, plus other prepped goodies – the combos are limited only by your imagination.

## COMBO 1

Healthy fish cakes
Pages 62–3

Pickles

White bean hummus
Page 86

Salad greens

**PLUS** capers, lemon, parsley, spring onion, yoghurt dressing, pepper

## COMBO 2

Healthy fish cakes Pages 62–3

Corn tortilla

Avocado

Salad greens

The simple one dressing Page 122

## COMBO 3

Healthy fish cakes Pages 62–3

Quinoa
Page 89

Diced capsicum

Spiralised carrot

Pomegranate seeds

Lemon + tahini dressing
Page 122

STEP 3 PUT IT TOGETHER

# Satay tofu crumble combos

Packed with calcium, tofu is an awesome source of your daily dose of that nutrient.
Pair with vegies, nuts and herbs for a fast and delicious meal.

## COMBO 1

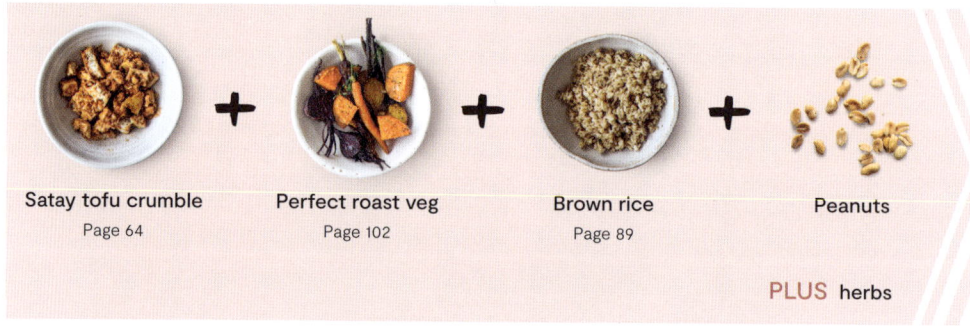

Satay tofu crumble + Perfect roast veg + Brown rice + Peanuts
Page 64 — Page 102 — Page 89

**PLUS** herbs

## COMBO 2

Satay tofu crumble + Miso eggplant + Broccoli + Cashews
Page 64 — Page 58

**PLUS** Thai basil

## COMBO 3

Satay tofu crumble + Roasted pumpkin mash + Miso + Miso + almond dressing + Cauliflower steak + Chopped almonds
Page 64 — Page 100 — — Page 123 — Page 56

162

STEP 3 PUT IT TOGETHER

# Cauliflower steak combos

These steaks make a great base for your favourite protein. Pile it up on top and add the dressing of your choice from pages 122–23.

## COMBO 1

Cauliflower steak
Page 56

+ Pea + almond pesto
Page 122

+ Poached egg
Page 45

+ Black pepper

PLUS herbs, salt, chilli oil

## COMBO 2

Cauliflower steak
Page 56

+ Pea + almond pesto Page 122

+ Tomatoes

+ Pine nuts

+ Milk-poached chicken Page 50

## COMBO 3

Cauliflower steak
Page 56

+ Lemon-grilled fish
Page 60

+ Salad greens

+ Lentil hummus
Page 86

+ Marinated chickpeas
Page 116

STEP 3 PUT IT TOGETHER

# Zucchini fritter combos

Eat zucchini fritters hot or cold. Use them as the base of a meal or crumble them on top of vegies, grains or salad greens. Add a tangy dressing for a contrast of flavour.

## COMBO 1

Zucchini fritters — Page 98 **+** Marinated chickpeas — Page 116 **+** The green one dressing — Page 123 **+** Julienned cucumber

**PLUS** pecans, pickled celery, fennel, carrot, onion, lemon wedges, coriander

## COMBO 2

Zucchini fritters — Page 98 **+** Lemon-grilled fish — Page 60 **+** Coriander **+** Teff — Page 89 **+** Vinaigrette — Page 120

## COMBO 3

Zucchini fritters — Page 98 **+** Feta **+** Roasted pumpkin mash — Page 100 **+** Pepper **+** Olive oil

STEP 3 PUT IT TOGETHER

# One-tray chicken combos

There are three types of seasoning for oven-baked chicken on pages 48–49, or use your own favourite. Once the chicken is cooked, add sweet or savoury accompaniments to keep it interesting for every meal. Some of my favourite additions include lime, mango and herbs.

## COMBO 1

One-tray chicken: lemon + rosemary
Pages 48–49

Coconut tzatziki dressing Page 123

Pickled celery Page 124–25

Olive oil

PLUS walnuts, apple, grapes, salad greens, herbs

## COMBO 2

One-tray chicken: spicy barbecue
Pages 48–49

Avocado

Mango

Tomatoes

Lime juice

Black beans

PLUS chilli

## COMBO 3

One-tray chicken: maple sesame
Pages 48–49

Brown rice
Page 89

Rocket

Pea + almond pesto Page 122

Tomatoes

Basil

PLUS almonds

STEP 3 PUT IT TOGETHER

# Hummus combos

You might say that I'm obsessed with hummus. How do I eat you?
Let me count the ways...

## COMBO 1

White bean hummus
Page 86

Nut butter falafel
Page 54

Radish

Vinaigrette
Page 120

PLUS tomatoes, black sesame seeds, salad greens, pomegranate seeds

## COMBO 2

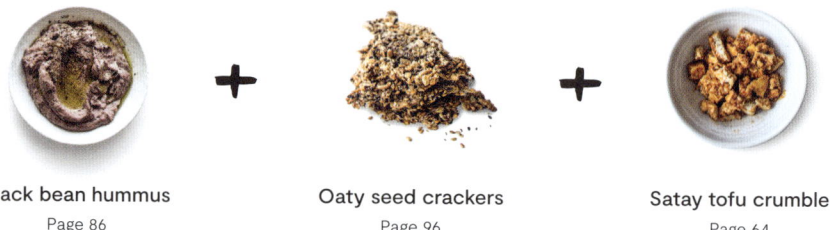

Black bean hummus
Page 86

Oaty seed crackers
Page 96

Satay tofu crumble
Page 64

## COMBO 3

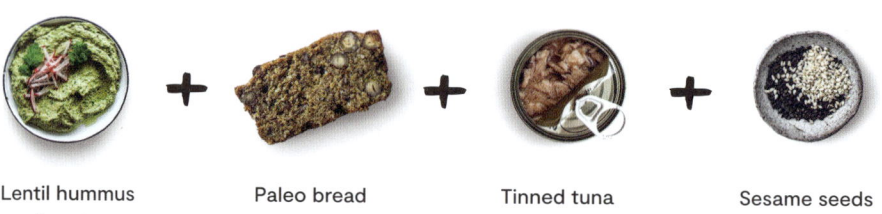

Lentil hummus
Page 86

Paleo bread
Page 90

Tinned tuna

Sesame seeds

STEP 3 PUT IT TOGETHER

# Oven-baked salmon combos

Salmon is rich in omega-3s, which have been shown to reduce inflammation in the gut.
I enjoy this fish a few times a week with fresh herbs, grains and spices.

## COMBO 1

Foolproof oven-baked salmon
Pages 42–43

Quinoa
Page 89

Moroccan spice mix

Pomegranate seeds

PLUS hazelnuts, raisins, herbs, vinaigrette

## COMBO 2

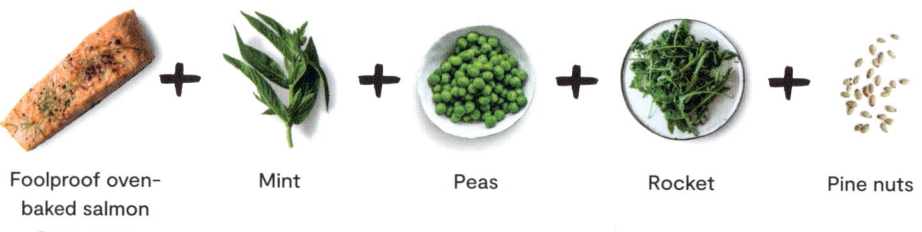

Foolproof oven-baked salmon
Pages 42–43

Mint

Peas

Rocket

Pine nuts

## COMBO 3

Foolproof oven-baked salmon
Pages 42–43

Cucumber

Avocado

Corn

Radish

Vinaigrette
Page 120

STEP 3 PUT IT TOGETHER

# Cooked prawn combos

I always keep cooked prawns in my freezer. They defrost quickly, and can be eaten cold or quickly heated through. They turn any salad, vegies or leftovers into a meal in a flash.

## COMBO 1

Cooked prawns (Page 25) + Corn + Avocado + Tomatoes

**PLUS** chilli flakes, fresh chilli, mango, black beans, lime, salad greens, herbs

## COMBO 2

Cooked prawns (Page 25) + The simple one dressing (Page 122) + Cucumber + Coriander + Lettuce cups + Lemon

## COMBO 3

Cooked prawns (Page 25) + Rice noodles + Lemon zest + Miso broth + Crushed peanuts + Mint

STEP 3 PUT IT TOGETHER

# Asian-style turkey mince combos

Forget takeaway food: just a few simple combos with this spicy Asian-style dish will have you assembling restaurant-quality dishes in no time.

## COMBO 1

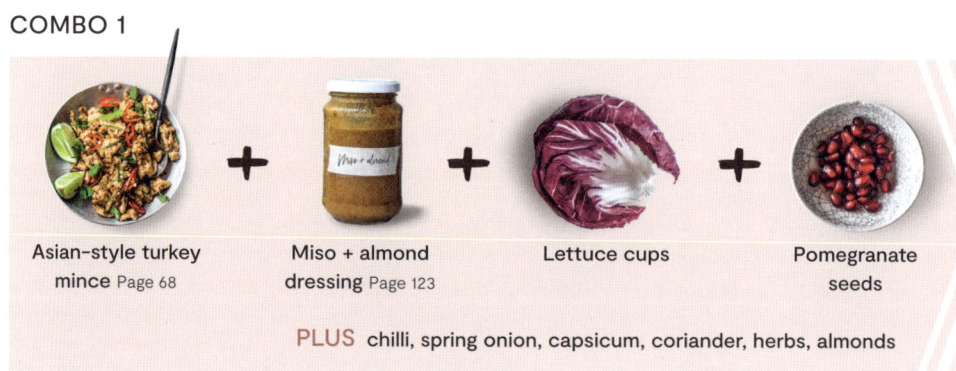

Asian-style turkey mince Page 68  +  Miso + almond dressing Page 123  +  Lettuce cups  +  Pomegranate seeds

PLUS chilli, spring onion, capsicum, coriander, herbs, almonds

## COMBO 2

Asian-style turkey mince Page 68  +  Roasted pumpkin mash Page 100  +  Marinated chickpeas Page 116  +  Sesame seeds  +  Broken toasted tortilla

## COMBO 3

Asian-style turkey mince Page 68  +  Brown rice Page 89  +  Poached egg Page 45  +  Dried chilli flakes  +  Honey

STEP 3 PUT IT TOGETHER

# Spiralised vegie combos

Whether you spiralise them yourself, or buy them already shredded from the supermarket (remember, shortcuts are totally OK!) these curly vegie strings make a nutritious and fun base for any meal. Steam them, add them to a stir-fry or eat them raw if you love that crunch.

## COMBO 1

Spiralised vegies + Lemon + tahini dressing Page 122 + Marinated chickpeas Page 116 + Avocado

PLUS sesame seeds, spring onion, parsley

## COMBO 2

Spiralised vegies + Rocket + Parmesan cheese + Pine nuts + Olive oil

## COMBO 3

Spiralised vegies + One-tray chicken Pages 48–49 + Coriander + Lemon + Cashews

STEP 3 PUT IT TOGETHER

# DIY muesli combos

I love to start a weekend with a bowl of peanutty chocolate muesli — and when you make your own mixture of muesli as a base, breakfast will never be the same again.

## COMBO 1

DIY muesli
Page 78

Cacao nibs

Peanuts

Cinnamon

**PLUS** buckwheat groats, freeze-dried banana, vanilla powder, toasted coconut

## COMBO 2

DIY muesli
Page 78

Almond milk

Fresh banana slices

Maple syrup

## COMBO 3

DIY muesli
Page 78

Chopped apple

Cinnamon

Warm macadamia milk

STEP 3 PUT IT TOGETHER

# Blender cookie dough combos

I know you probably just want to spoon this sweet treat straight into your mouth (no judgement) but you can take it to the NEXT LEVEL with these additions.

## COMBO 1

Blender cookie dough Page 140 + Salted caramel Page 132 + Blended frozen banana + Cacao nibs

**PLUS** medjool dates, pistachios, sea salt flakes

## COMBO 2

Blender cookie dough Page 140 + Apple slices + Raisins + Nutmeg

## COMBO 3

Blender cookie dough Page 140 + Blended frozen banana + Tahini + Cinnamon

STEP 3 PUT IT TOGETHER

# Frozen banana combos

Not only are bananas loaded with fibre and vitamins, they're the perfect blender-buddy for smoothies and creamy desserts. I have heaps of them in my freezer year-round. Tip: peel and slice them before freezing: it's so much easier.

## COMBO 1

Frozen banana + Peanuts + Cacao nibs + Miso

PLUS almond milk, peanut butter

## COMBO 2

Frozen banana + Avocado + Lime + Kale

PLUS coconut milk

## COMBO 3

Frozen banana + Roasted pumpkin mash Page 100 + Maple syrup + Cinnamon

PLUS coconut milk, nutmeg, oats

STEP 3 PUT IT TOGETHER

# Supergrain combos

Packed with fibre, wholegrains form the base for dishes that help keep you feeling satisfied and help control your blood-sugar levels too.

## COMBO 1

Freekeh
Page 89

\+ Sticky and sugarless caramelised onions
Page 104

\+ Roasted pumpkin mash with miso
Page 100

\+ Poached egg
Page 45

**PLUS** rocket

## COMBO 2

Freekeh
Page 89

\+ Brown rice
Page 89

\+ Toasted coconut flakes

\+ Garlic

\+ Ginger

**PLUS** coconut milk, sea salt

## COMBO 3

Freekeh
Page 89

\+ Sticky and sugarless caramelised onions
Page 104

\+ Teff
Page 89

\+ Foolproof oven-baked salmon Pages 42–43

\+ Mint

**PLUS** feta, parsley, chopped dates

STEP 3 PUT IT TOGETHER

# Lemon-grilled fish combos

Any white-fleshed fish will work well here. Barramundi is found throughout South-east Asia and northern Australia, and it's a great option. Pair this tasty seafood with healthy fats and fibre for a balanced meal.

## COMBO 1

Lemon-grilled fish — Page 60 + Vinaigrette — Page 120 + Shaved radish + Coriander

PLUS carrot, capsicum, spring onions, salad greens, grilled lemon halves

## COMBO 2

Lemon-grilled fish Page 60 + Avocado + Parsley + Lime + Hazelnuts + Tortilla

## COMBO 3

Lemon-grilled fish — Page 60 + Pea + almond pesto — Page 122 + Perfect roast veg — Page 102

188

STEP 3 PUT IT TOGETHER

# Salted choc banana bread combos

You will be amazed at the flavour combinations that taste great on this rich chocolate dessert loaf.

## COMBO 1

Salted chocolate banana bread
Page 130

\+

Sliced banana

\+

Salted caramel
Page 132

\+

Cinnamon

**PLUS** chopped almonds, chia seeds, almond butter

## COMBO 2

Salted chocolate banana bread Page 130

\+

Ricotta cheese

\+

Honey

\+

Pistachios

## COMBO 3

Salted chocolate banana bread Page 130

\+

Mashed raspberries

\+

Peanut butter

STEP 3 PUT IT TOGETHER

# Flax waffle combos

Toast up these waffles and top them with savoury or sweet flavours for breakfast, lunch or dessert.

## COMBO 1

Flax waffles + Boiled eggs + The green one dressing + Pepper
Page 92      Page 44      Page 123

**PLUS** avocado, chopped kale, crumbled seed crackers

## COMBO 2

Flax waffles + Milk-poached chicken + Lemon + tahini dressing + Rocket
Page 92      Page 50                  Page 122

## COMBO 3

Flax waffles + Cinnamon + Blueberries + Blender cookie dough
Page 92                                  Page 140

STEP 3 PUT IT TOGETHER

# Milk-poached chicken combos

Add different sauces, spices and textures to make this tender chicken even more delicious.

## COMBO 1

Milk-poached chicken Page 50 + Buckwheat Page 89 + Miso broth + Coriander

**PLUS** spring onion, black sesame seeds, herbs

## COMBO 2

Milk-poached chicken Page 50 + Cauliflower steak Page 56 + Pea + almond pesto Page 122 + Pomegranate seeds

## COMBO 3

Milk-poached chicken Page 50 + The simple one dressing Page 122 + Salad greens + Chopped avocado + Toasted coconut flakes

STEP 3 PUT IT TOGETHER

# Roasted pumpkin combos

Roasted pumpkin is naturally sweet. I love to pair it with salty flavours for balance.

## COMBO 1

Roasted pumpkin + Feta + Honey + Rocket
Page 100

**PLUS** pumpkin seeds, spinach, pepper, rosemary

## COMBO 2

Roasted pumpkin + Lime + Soy sauce + Peanut butter
Page 100

blend and heat with enough coconut milk to make a soup

## COMBO 3

Roasted pumpkin + Satay tofu crumble + Broccoli + Sesame oil + Spring onion
Page 100    Page 64

STEP 3 PUT IT TOGETHER

# Miso eggplant combos

Pair this salty–sweet roasted vegetable with vegies or your favourite protein to make a simple umami delight.

## COMBO 1

Miso eggplant
Page 58

+ Spiralised vegies

+ Pickled eggs
Page 47

+ Brown rice
Page 89

**PLUS** spring onion, herbs, pickled ginger, chilli, sesame seeds, brown rice, soy sauce, tofu

## COMBO 2

Miso eggplant
Page 58

+ Poached egg
Page 45

+ Spring onion

+ Green beans

+ Radish

+ The green one dressing Page 123

## COMBO 3

Miso eggplant
Page 58

+ Spicy beef mince
Page 70

+ Avocado

+ Cauliflower rice

STEP 3 PUT IT TOGETHER

# Marinated chickpea combos

Packed with protein and fibre, these little powerhouses don't need much else to make a sensational dish. Add some healthy fat (such as avocado, feta or salmon) for a winning nutrient combo.

## COMBO 1

Marinated chickpeas
Page 116

+

White bean hummus
Page 86

+

Feta

+

Tomatoes

PLUS corn, coriander, herbs, dried chilli flakes

## COMBO 2

Marinated chickpeas
Page 116

+

Salad greens

+

One-tray chicken
Pages 48–49

+

Avocado

## COMBO 3

Marinated chickpeas
Page 116

+

Foolproof oven-baked salmon Pages 42–43

+

Roasted pumpkin
Page 100

+

Parsley

STEP 3 PUT IT TOGETHER

# Basic chicken meatloaf combos

I use slices of meatloaf like toast. Grill and spread with avo, feta, cottage cheese — whatever you love! Or crumble the meatloaf into a salad for extra protein.

## COMBO 1

Basic chicken meatloaf Pages 52–53 + The green one dressing Page 123 + Avocado + Spring onions

**PLUS** cherry tomatoes, herbs, lime, olive oil, chilli flakes

## COMBO 2

Basic chicken meatloaf Pages 52–53 + Perfect roast veg Page 102 + Lemon + tahini dressing Page 122 + Basil

## COMBO 3

Basic chicken meatloaf Pages 52–53 + Green beans + Roasted pumpkin mash Page 100 + Feta

# Index

**A**
additives  29
amino acids  17
anchovy, broccoli and pear soup  118
antioxidants  23
apple, goat's cheese and sage quiche  108
Asian-style turkey mince  68
    combos  176
avocados  17

**B**
baking paper/foil  36
baking trays  36
balanced meals  15, 16–19, 96
bananas  31
    frozen banana combos  184
    salted chocolate banana bread  130
basic meals  11
batch-making  11, 77
berries  26, 28, 29
    frozen  32
black pepper  20
blender cookie dough  140
    combos  182
bliss balls  26
    DIY  146
blood-sugar levels  16, 23
boss meal  18–19
bread
    one-bowl nutty paleo bread  90–91
    salted chocolate banana bread  130

**C**
Canadian pumpkin pie  110
capers  23
caramel, salted  132
carbohydrates (carbs)  16–17, 18
cardamom, chocolate and cherry tray-baked oats  134
carrots  29
cauliflower pizza bases  112
cauliflower steaks  56–57
    combos  164
celery sticks  29
cereal bars, smoky chocolate  84
cheese  32
chicken
    basic chicken meatloaf combos  202
    basic meatloaf  52
    chicken crust meatza  72
    milk-poached  50
    one-tray, three ways  48–49
    one-tray chicken combos  168
    poached breasts  30
    roasted  28
    seasonings  49
    sliced meatloaf  32
    soup  51
chickpeas, marinated  116
chillies  20
chocolate
    cardamom, chocolate and cherry tray-baked oats  134
    chocolate chip cookies, four ingredients  148
    chocolate proghurt  144
    salted choc banana bread  130
    smoky chocolate cereal bars  84
chopping board  36
cinnamon  23
citrus  23, 24
coconut fudge bites  144
coconut oil  17, 142
coconut tzatziki  123
complex carbs  16, 18
containers  34–35
    glass or plastic  34
    recycling  34
cookies
    blender cookie dough  140
    chocolate chip cookies, four ingredients  148
    nana cookies  144
    rosemary and tahini cookies  94
coriander  23
crackers
    oaty seed crackers  96
    sweet crackers  144
cream  32
crumbles
    fruit crumble duo  142
    satay tofu crumble  64, 162

**D**
dressings  18, 23, 24, 122–23
    with citrus  23
    the green one  123
    prepped, in fridge  30
    the simple one  122

**E**
eggs
    boiled  26, 44
    hard-boiled  26, 28
    meal-prepped  44–45
    peeling  44
    pickled  46–47
    poached  45
    poached egg combos  152
    sweet potatoes with baked eggs  74
equipment  36–37

**F**
falafel
    combos  156
    flavourings  54
    nut butter  54
fats  16, 17, 18
fibre  80, 86
fish  60
    fish cake combos  160
    healthy fish cakes  62–63
    lemon-grilled fish  60
    oven-baked salmon combos  172
    Thai-style fish cakes  63
    *see also* salmon

five days of overnight oats  80
flavour bombs  18, 20, 23
    chicken meatloaf  53
    falafel  54
    paleo bread  91
flax waffles  92
    combos  192
food assembly  10–11, 30
food fatigue  13
food labels  29
foolproof oven-baked
  salmon  42
freezer  33
    food expands in  33, 86
    prepping  32–33
fridge, as salad bar  30–31
fruit crumble duo  142

G
garlic  20
    chopped  33
ginger  33
glucose  16
grains  24, 88–89, 186
    combos  186
    cooked  33
grater  36
gravlax, salt-cured  40

H
healthy fish cakes  62–63
    combos  160
healthy meals  6, 8
hummus
    combos  170
    DIY hummus  86–87
    with vegies  26, 29

I
icetrays  32, 36

J
jerky  29

K
kitchen knives  36, 37
kitchen scissors  36

L
leftover vegetable bake  114
lemon and tahini dressing  123

lemon-grilled fish  60
    combos  188
lemons, waxed  61
loaf tin  36

M
macronutrients  16–17
marinated chickpeas  116
    combos  200
meal planning  12–15
meal prep  8, 10–11, 14–15, 30, 102
measuring jug  36
microwaves  25
milk-poached chicken  50
    combos  194
minerals  16, 20
miso  20
miso and almond dressing  123
miso eggplant  58
    combos  198
mix and match buffet-style  15
mixing bowls  36
mud slice, raspberry and peanut
  butter  136
muesli
    combos  180
    DIY muesli  78–79
    how to eat  79
    toasted  79
multitasking  14, 43

N
nana cookies  144
notebook  12–13
nutrition  16–17
nuts  26, 28, 32
    nut butter falafel  54
    nut clusters  138
    nut milk  24
    nutty paleo bread  90–91

O
oats
    cardamom, chocolate and
      cherry tray-baked  134
    oat sachets  29
    oaty seed crackers  96
    prepping  80
    sweet/savoury  80
one-bowl nutty paleo bread
  90–91

onions
    chopped  33
    spring onions  23, 70
    sticky and sugarless
      caramelised onions  104
oven-baked salmon  42
    combos  172
oysters  29

P
paleo bread  32
paprika  23
pea and almond pesto  122
peanut butter ice cream  144
peelings  31
pepper  20
pickles
    quick  124–25
    vegetables  124
pie crusts, sweet and savoury
  gluten-free  106
pineapple ice  144
pink salt  20
pizza
    cauliflower pizza bases  112
    chicken crust meatza  72
    toppings  74
poached egg combos  152
potassium  20
prawns
    cooked and frozen  25
    cooked prawn combos  174
prepping *see* meal prep
proghurt  26, 144
protein bars/balls  28
protein powders  26
proteins  16, 17, 18, 29, 38
    prepping  38
pumpkin
    Canadian pumpkin pie  110
    roasted pumpkin combos  196
    whole roasted pumpkin
  100–01

Q
quiche, apple, goat's cheese and
  sage  108

R
raspberry and peanut butter mud
  slice  136

recycling  34
rice  16
    sachets  24
    vegetable rice  25
roasting  14
root vegies  14
rosemary and tahini cookies  94

## S
salad bags  29
salad bar
    in fridge  30–31
salad prepping  30
salmon
    medium-rare  42
    oven-baked  42
    oven-baked combos  172
    teriyaki glaze  43
salmon gravlax  40
    combos  154
salt  20
salted caramel  132
salted choc banana bread  130
    combos  190
satay tofu crumble  64
    combos  162
sauces  14, 24
seeds  32
shortcuts  10, 15, 24–25
silicone spatula  37
simple carbs  16
smoky chocolate cereal bars  84
smoky turkey rissoles  66
    combos  158
smoothie bags  33
    DIY  82–83
    resealable  82
snacks  11, 26, 30
soup
    anchovy, broccoli and pear  118
    chicken  51
sour cream  32
spice mixes  24
spicy beef mince  70
spiralised vegies  25
    combos  178
spiraliser  37
spring onions  23, 70
sriracha  23

sticky and sugarless caramelised onions  104
stock  25
stock cubes  25, 80
storage containers  34–35
supergrains  88–89
supermarket saviours  28–29
sweet crackers  144
sweet potatoes with baked eggs  74
sweet and savoury freezer truffles  129
sweet and savoury gluten-free pie crusts  106
sweet treats, with two ingredients  144–45

## T
teriyaki glaze, sugar-free  43
time-saving  13, 14, 24–25, 31, 102, 272
tofu
    hard  29
    satay tofu crumble  64
tongs  37
toppings
    for oats  80, 134
    for sweet potatoes  74
trail mix  24
    DIY  126
truffles, sweet and savoury  129
tuna, tinned  29
turkey
    Asian-style turkey mince  68
    smoky turkey rissoles  66

## U
unsaturated fats  17

## V
variety, in food  14, 16
vegetable rice  25
vegetables
    frozen  32
    with hummus  26, 29
    leftover vegetable bake  114
    the perfect roast veg  102
    pickled  124
    prepping  30
    reheating  102
    root vegies  14

spiralised  25
spiralised combos  178
vinaigrettes, DIY  120–21
vitamin C  23, 25
vitamins  16, 17

## W
waffles  92
whisk  37
white vinegar  124

## Y
yoghurt
    chocolate proghurt  144
    plain Greek  28
    proghurt  26, 144
    vanilla maple  110

## Z
zester  37
zucchini fritters  98
    combos  166

# Thank you

Firstly, a HUGE thank you to you, for picking up this book and for continuing to love what I do. I couldn't share my passion for simple, healthy food without your incredible support, so thank you for inviting me into your living room / kitchen / bed and reading this. Never stop investing in yourself and your health.

To the entire team at Murdoch (both in Australia and in the UK). You all deserve the biggest bloody high five and collective group squeeze. I am grateful to everyone who had these pages cross your desk and annoyingly fill up your inbox. There were so many of you working tirelessly behind the scenes to pull this together and I appreciate every single one of you. If nothing else, I hope this book makes a useful doorstop or computer monitor stand.

Dad. You have helped me become the hero of my own story. There is nothing I can do to repay you for your relentless, unwavering support and motivation at every turn. I love you.

Lee (@thiswildlinglife__), you are the best girlfriend and confidant a girl could ever wish for. Thank you for listening to me every damn day, celebrating all the highs and picking me up when I'm down. Through heartbreaks, book deals, detailed discussions on my digestive system, and everything in between. You inspire me every day to hustle hard and aim higher. I love you to the moon and back.

Jesse (@jadammms), from changing your flights to hang with a stranger in New Zealand, to all the incredible travel memories thus far, it's been one epic journey. Thank you for bringing a bit more balance to my life, and for inspiring the pumpkin pie recipe with those 10 amazing days in the Canadian Rockies. You have made memories for a lifetime that I will never forget. I'm still coming down off that sugar high.

Sash (@livewithoutlabels), thank you for your consistent patience, nutrition tutoring in my time of need, incredible photography and everything in between. I'm so blessed you saved me that seat on my first day of lectures.

Jane M, from listening to my pitch (and telling me to come back with a better one – you lovely hard-ass!), to developing my idea and trusting me to shoot my own food. You had faith in this project from the word GO and I am grateful you took that chance to make magic with me. Thank you for your guidance and support.

Meg, for turning my images and words into a piece of art, being so on board with my vision from day one, and for the epic hand modelling and giggles on set. You have taken this book to the next level and created something I will still be proud of when I'm old and grey.

Jane P, thank you for your unwavering patience in this journey and the hundreds of emails you had to send that kept me on target and in line to get this project done. Your calm and collected way of getting things done got us over the line. Phew. You deserve a medal.

Sarah (@msmayohnaise) for your consistently solid work in my kitchen day after day. Not only did you follow my sometimes questionable recipes that needed a little more testing, but you kept me sane during a very intense four weeks. You even made it hella fun (with a little help from Sam Smith too). I look forward to the day we work together again, gal. I wouldn't have done this without you, and would probably be another 10 kilos heavier.

To all my loved ones, for dealing with me during deadlines, late nights and for giving me words of encouragement when I needed them the most. Your unconditional support knows no bounds – thank you.

Published in 2026 by Murdoch Books, an imprint of Allen & Unwin
Originally published as The Fit Foodie Meal Prep Plan in 2019

Murdoch Books Australia
Cammeraygal Country
83 Alexander Street
Crows Nest NSW 2065
Phone: +61 (0)2 8425 0100
murdochbooks.com.au
info@murdochbooks.com.au

Murdoch Books UK
Ormond House
26–27 Boswell Street
London WC1N 3JZ
Phone: +44 (0) 20 8785 5995
murdochbooks.co.uk
info@murdochbooks.co.uk

For corporate orders and custom publishing, contact our business development team at salesenquiries@murdochbooks.com.au

Publisher: Jane Morrow
Editorial manager: Jane Price
Design manager: Megan Pigott
Designer: Sarah Odgers
Editor: Melody Lord
Photographer: Sally O'Neill (except pages 2, 7 by Sasha Leong, 208 by Ella Dice at Dream Creative)
Stylist: Vivien Walsh
Home economist: Sarah Mayoh
Commissioning editor (2026 edition):
  Justin Wolfers
Production manager: Natalie Crouch

Text and internal photography
© Sally O'Neill 2026 (except pages 2, 7, by Sasha Leong, 208 by Ella Dice at Dream Creative)
The moral right of the author has been asserted.
Design © Murdoch Books 2026
Photography © Sally O'Neill 2026
Cover photography © Rob Palmer 2026

Murdoch Books acknowledges the Traditional Owners of the Country on which we live and work. We pay our respects to all Aboriginal and Torres Strait Islander Elders, past and present.

EU Authorised Representative: Easy Access System Europe, Mustamäe tee 50, 10621 Tallinn, Estonia, gpsr.requests@easproject.com

All rights reserved. No part of this publication may be reproduced, stored in a retrieval system or transmitted in any form or by any means, electronic, mechanical, photocopying, recording or otherwise, without the prior written permission of the publisher.

Colour reproduction by Splitting Image Colour Studio Pty Ltd, Wantirna, Victoria
Printed in China by C&C Offset Printing Co., Ltd.

OVEN GUIDE: You may find cooking times vary depending on the oven and oven setting you are using. For fan-forced (convection) ovens, as a general rule, set the oven temperature to 20°C (25–50°F) lower than indicated in the recipe.

TABLESPOON MEASURES: We have used 20 ml (4 teaspoon) tablespoon measures. If you are using a 15 ml (3 teaspoon) tablespoon add an extra teaspoon of the ingredient for each tablespoon specified.

ISBN 9 781 76150 145 6

10 9 8 7 6 5 4 3 2 1

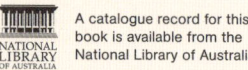
A catalogue record for this book is available from the National Library of Australia

MIX
Paper | Supporting responsible forestry
FSC® C008047